# Novel Design and the Applications of Smart-M3 Platform in the Internet of Things:

## Emerging Research and Opportunities

Dmitry Korzun
*Petrozavodsk State University (PetrSU), Russia*

Alexey Kashevnik
*St. Petersburg Institute for Informatics and Automation of the Russian Academy of Sciences (SPIIRAS), Russia & ITMO University, Russia*

Sergey Balandin
*FRUCT Oy, Finland & St. Petersburg State University of Aerospace Instrumentation (SUAI), Russia*

A volume in the Advances in Web Technologies and Engineering (AWTE) Book Series

Published in the United States of America by
  IGI Global
  Information Science Reference (an imprint of IGI Global)
  701 E. Chocolate Avenue
  Hershey PA, USA 17033
  Tel: 717-533-8845
  Fax:  717-533-8661
  E-mail: cust@igi-global.com
  Web site: http://www.igi-global.com

Library of Congress Cataloging-in-Publication Data

Names: Korzun, Dmitry, author.
Title: Novel design and the applications of smart-M3 platform in the
  internet of things : emerging research and opportunities / by Dmitry
  Korzun, Alexey Kashevnik, and Sergey Balandin.
Description: Hershey, PA : Information Science Reference, [2017] | Includes
  bibliographical references and index.
Identifiers: LCCN 2017008481| ISBN 9781522526537 (hardcover) | ISBN
  9781522526544 (ebook)
Subjects:  LCSH: Internet of things.
Classification: LCC TK5105.8857 .K67 2017 | DDC 004.67/8--dc23 LC record available at https://
lccn.loc.gov/2017008481

This book is published in the IGI Global book series Advances in Web Technologies and
Engineering (AWTE) (ISSN: 2328-2762; eISSN: 2328-2754)

British Cataloguing in Publication Data
A Cataloguing in Publication record for this book is available from the British Library.

All work contributed to this book is new, previously-unpublished material.
The views expressed in this book are those of the authors, but not necessarily of the publisher.

For electronic access to this publication, please contact: eresources@igi-global.com.

# Advances in Web Technologies and Engineering (AWTE) Book Series

ISSN:2328-2762
EISSN:2328-2754

Editor-in-Chief: Ghazi I. Alkhatib, The Hashemite University, Jordan & David C. Rine, George Mason University, USA

## MISSION

The **Advances in Web Technologies and Engineering (AWTE) Book Series** aims to provide a platform for research in the area of Information Technology (IT) concepts, tools, methodologies, and ethnography, in the contexts of global communication systems and Web engineered applications. Organizations are continuously overwhelmed by a variety of new information technologies, many are Web based. These new technologies are capitalizing on the widespread use of network and communication technologies for seamless integration of various issues in information and knowledge sharing within and among organizations. This emphasis on integrated approaches is unique to this book series and dictates cross platform and multidisciplinary strategy to research and practice.

The **Advances in Web Technologies and Engineering (AWTE) Book Series** seeks to create a stage where comprehensive publications are distributed for the objective of bettering and expanding the field of web systems, knowledge capture, and communication technologies. The series will provide researchers and practitioners with solutions for improving how technology is utilized for the purpose of a growing awareness of the importance of web applications and engineering.

## COVERAGE

- Knowledge Structure, Classification, and Search Algorithms or Engines
- Case Studies Validating Web-Based IT Solutions
- Information Filtering and Display Adaptation Techniques for Wireless Devices
- Integrated Heterogeneous and Homogeneous Workflows and Databases Within and Across Organizations and With Suppliers and Customers
- Strategies for Linking Business Needs and IT
- Software Agent-Based Applications
- IT readiness and Technology Transfer Studies
- Data Analytics for Business and Government Organizations
- Web Systems Performance Engineering Studies
- Data and Knowledge Capture and Quality Issues

IGI Global is currently accepting manuscripts for publication within this series. To submit a proposal for a volume in this series, please contact our Acquisition Editors at Acquisitions@igi-global.com or visit: http://www.igi-global.com/publish/.

# Titles in this Series

*For a list of additional titles in this series, please visit:*
*http://www.igi-global.com/book-series/advances-web-technologies-engineering/37158*

***Developing Metadata Application Profiles***
Mariana Curado Malta (Polytechnic of Oporto, Portugal & Algoritmi Center, University of Minho, Portugal) Ana Alice Baptista (Algoritmi Center, University of Minho, Portugal) and Paul Walk (University of Edinburh, UK)
Information Science Reference ● ©2017 ● 248pp ● H/C (ISBN: 9781522522218) ● US $170.00

***Game Theory Solutions for the Internet of Things Emerging Research and Opporunities***
Sungwook Kim (Sogang University, South Korea)
Information Science Reference ● ©2017 ● 221pp ● H/C (ISBN: 9781522519522) ● US $130.00

***Design Solutions for Improving Website Quality and Effectiveness***
G. Sreedhar (Rashtriya Sanskrit Vidyapeetha (Deemed University), India)
Information Science Reference ● ©2016 ● 423pp ● H/C (ISBN: 9781466697645) ● US $220.00

***Handbook of Research on Redesigning the Future of Internet Architectures***
Mohamed Boucadair (France Télécom, France) and Christian Jacquenet (France Télécom, France)
Information Science Reference ● ©2015 ● 621pp ● H/C (ISBN: 9781466683716) ● US $345.00

***Artificial Intelligence Technologies and the Evolution of Web 3.0***
Tomayess Issa (Curtin University, Australia) and Pedro Isaías (Universidade Aberta (Portuguese Open University), Portugal)
Information Science Reference ● ©2015 ● 422pp ● H/C (ISBN: 9781466681477) ● US $225.00

***Frameworks, Methodologies, and Tools for Developing Rich Internet Applications***
Giner Alor-Hernández (Instituto Tecnológico de Orizaba, Mexico) Viviana Yarel Rosales-Morales (Instituto Tecnológico de Orizaba, Mexico) and Luis Omar Colombo-Mendoza (Instituto Tecnológico de Orizaba, Mexico)
Information Science Reference ● ©2015 ● 349pp ● H/C (ISBN: 9781466664371) ● US $195.00

*For an enitre list of titles in this series, please visit:*
*http://www.igi-global.com/book-series/advances-web-technologies-engineering/37158*

701 East Chocolate Avenue, Hershey, PA 17033, USA
Tel: 717-533-8845 x100 ● Fax: 717-533-8661
E-Mail: cust@igi-global.com ● www.igi-global.com

# Table of Contents

# Foreword

Everything is becoming "smart", or "smarter"—our phones have evolved from voice communication to fully fledged computers integrating with the host of devices and the environment. Even simple devices such as switches and light bulbs now exist not just in the physical world but as entities within a much larger internet.

The spaces we exist and interact in have many, overlapping and interacting virtual counterparts: "Smart Spaces". These spaces enable us to communicate, learn and interact in ways and means we have not so far experienced. They will allow new business, new services and redefine our very perception of our environment as a whole. Even today with the advent of IoT—enabled by the Internet and mobile communication—we are starting to see environment not just react to us but to evolve along with us.

The concept of "Smart Spaces" as being presented in this book is the culmination of many aspects of research: agent technologies, Semantic Web, mobile technologies, semantics, ontologies, communication, AI, learning - just to merely scratch the surface of the sheer number of interacting technologies.

In some ways "Smart Spaces" is a very old technology and can trace its roots back to early work on agent systems and the "actor model" and even early AI itself. These early implementations had problems and raised many interesting research questions such as how to represent information, how to transmit information, how to distribute information leading to huge technological leaps. Indeed, the work here stemmed from early work on Semantic Web and its integration with the pre-App model mobile infrastructure.

Interestingly one of the ideas of Smart Spaces early on was to challenge the idea of applications itself. One might argue that we lost to the App model but this itself might be seen as an inevitable pre-cursor to the idea that mobile devices, and even any device could host and even be an "App" in its own right.

As apps have proliferated so had the necessity for apps to communicate with each other and their environment. As the reader might perceive these are the very problems addressed in early research but only now finding a wider application.

Indeed, the work and research being presented here is itself just one point on a long sometimes disruptive, sometimes incremental path of discovery and realization of what we really need to live in a "Smart World". We are in effect continually learning what it means to be "smart."

The authors in this book are not just recording their work, their research and their vision but honouring all the past research and setting out the Future.

*Ian Oliver*
*Nokia Bell Labs, USA*

# Preface

The Internet of Things (IoT) is a fast-growing industry that is going to have huge impact on world's economy and life of ordinary people. The users demand smart services that go beyond existing web-like design, as it cannot provide satisfactory coupling and automatic composition of tasks when a user needs it. The IoT technologies evolve to a substrate for resource interconnection and convergence. This book summarizes the main findings of our research on design of a new generation of smart services. In particular, we focus on distributed Smart Spaces architecture. We illustrate features and advantages of this architecture by using the Smart-M3 platform. Smart-M3 is currently shaping into an open source technology for creating smart spaces with focus on development of smart services for various application domains.

A smart space is deployed in an IoT-enabled computing environment, creating an infrastructure for application to construct and deliver value-added services based on cooperative activity of environment participants, either human or machines. The book describes the suit of concept models, programming techniques, application development tools that make the Smart-M3 platform a valid technology of the today's Internet. The description is illustrated and referenced with several already implemented application case studies from such topical domains as collaborative work, social networking, transport logistics, mobile e-tourism, mobile health and wellbeing, and industrial Internet. the spectrum of applications that can be developed using the Smart Spaces concept is very wide. Variants of possible services are only limited by our imagination. These domains were selected based on our more than ten years' experience of research and development for Smart Spaces. This experience is reflected by several dozens of publications, the most essential ones are listed in the reference sections of the chapters.

One can find a lot of publications for Internet of Things, smart environments, and smart services. There is no reference book that discusses features of the distributed Smart Spaces architecture. Also, there is no book on the

Smart-M3 platform, which would present the latest technological aspects for the application development. This was the main motivation for us to prepare complete survey of the existing work in this area. The book fills the missing gap in the current IoT literature for students, researchers, and engineers. The main goal of the book is to describe the most important achievements of the Smart-M3 platform. They cover fundamental issues in development of smart spaces based applications for emerging Internet of Things environments. The book is illustrated by examples and case studies to help the understanding as well as include an extensive list of references on recent publications.

The material exposition of this book is organized as follows. Chapter 1 starts an introduction to the field and provides recent trends in IoT industry, user experience and expectation about services, motivating applications.

In Chapters 2 and 3, we discuss the M3 architecture for smart spaces, which aims at enabling advanced services on top of IoT environments. Service construction is based on information sharing with cooperative knowledge processing by participants themselves (either human or machines). This approach supports localization and interconnection of available resources, their semantics, and information-driven programming over this dynamic knowledge corpus. The settings of IoT environments play an essential practical role, influencing the way how a smart space and its applications are deployed on the existing networked equipment of a given IoT environment. We consider the Smart-M3 platform that forms an open source technology for creating M3-based smart spaces (M3 spaces) as heterogeneous dynamic multi-agent system with multi-device, multi-vendor, multi-domain participation. The agents are of restricted autonomy and focused on the knowledge processing function.

Chapter 4 introduces selected Smart-M3 techniques for application developers. The aspect of shared semantic information management becomes essential for service construction, and we describe techniques how implement this management in a smart space. A question of what is a smart service compared with regular service is still debatable, and we describe techniques how implement various intelligence attributes in services constructed and delivered in M3 spaces.

Chapter 5 emphasizes application issues of the presented technology. We study six topical application domains: collaborative work environments. These case studies demonstrate a possible spectrum of programming techniques and the ways of "thinking". Actually, variants of possible services are only limited by our imagination. The provided application case studies serve as reference models for smart space based application development.

# Acknowledgment

The scientific content of this book is primarily composed of the research results that have been developed within concurrent activity of the following projects, which are financially supported by the Ministry of Education and Science of the Russian Federation and by the Russian Fund for Basic Research (RFBR) (the projects are listed in chronological order).

Project no. 1481 *Methods of programming for service-oriented intelligent systems based on ontological models of interaction in heterogeneous computing environments of Internet of Things,* from the basic part of state research assignment # 2014/154 for 2014-2016 (implementing organization: PetrSU).

Project no. 2.2336.2014/K *Methods for ontology-driven development and intelligent Internet technologies for semantic services of the next generation in the area of cultural tourism,* from the project part of state research assignment for 2014-2016 (implementing organization: PetrSU).

Project no. 14-07-00252 *Methods for construction, maintenance and management of smart spaces content,* from RFBR for 2014-2016 (implementation organization: PetrSU).

Grant 074-U01 Leading Russian Federation Universities support for increasing their competitiveness in leading international research and development organizations from Russian Federation, 2014-2020 (implementing organization: ITMO University).

Project no. 16-07-00462 *Development of methodology and models for context-driven knowledge sharing for service-oriented decision support systems,* from RFBR for 2016-2018 (implementing organization: SPIIRAS).

Project no. 16-29-04349 *Theoretical and technological foundations for ontology-oriented mobile robots interaction in dynamically formed hybrid coalitions,* from RFBR for 2016-2018 (implementing organization: SPIIRAS).

Project no. 16-29-12866 *Theoretical and technological foundations for context-oriented collective interaction of scientific and technological expert networks participants during innovation formation,* from RFBR for 2016-2018 (implementing organization: SPIIRAS).

Project no. 2.5124.2017 *Modeling and Programming Fundamentals of Information-Driven Interaction in Socio-Cyber-Physical Systems for Internet of Things and Big Data,* from the basic part of state research assignment for 2017-2019 (implementing organization: PetrSU).

Project no. 089-02D (8.4048.2017) *Architecture and development methods of distributed computing and information systems for next generation of integrated modular avionics,* from the project part of state research assignment for 2017-2019 (implementing organization: SUAI).

Chapter 1

# Introduction to Smart Environments

## ABSTRACT

*Now the Internet of Things (IoT) is growing fast into a large industry with huge potential economic impact expected in near future. The IoT technology evolves to a substrate for resource interconnection and convergence. The users' needs go beyond the existing web-like services, which do not provide satisfactory coupling and automatic composition when the user tries to solve tasks from her/his everyday life. New generation of services (named "smart services") emerges. In this chapter, we introduce the problem of effective use of the multitude of IoT-enabled devices and other digital resources that now surround our lives. The devices support and assist human by provision of digital services. This is the key objective of a smart environment. Our focus is on such a particular class of smart environments as smart spaces. This class targets IoT-enabled computing environments, where a smart space is created and then provides an infrastructure for applications to construct and deliver value-added services based on cooperative activity of environment participants, either human or machines.*

## INTRODUCTION

We are already surrounded by huge number of various devices. These devices serve different purposes; they have some measuring capabilities (sensor devices), data processing capabilities (processing devices), and possibility

DOI: 10.4018/978-1-5225-2653-7.ch001

to influence the environment (environment control devices). Some of the devices have only one of these capabilities, e.g., sensors, some combine all three functions, i.e., such devices are called smart systems. Most important is that our living environment is changing very fast by the process of total digitalization.

Our lives are changing, thanks to the services delivered by surrounding devices. For example, a smart TV can record our preferred shows. A refrigerator can control what food is missing and remind to buy it by printing a shopping list or sending a text message to the preconfigured phone or email. Smart home sensors and actuators can keep most comfortable temperature in our house, while also optimizing the expenses, e.g., by using most of energy when it has the lowest price. Nevertheless, what is still missing is a scalable ecosystem that enables efficient co-working of all surrounding devices, everywhere at any time.

There have been many attempts to build such ecosystems. A number of studies on various specific topics has been presented recently, see examples in (Korzun, Borodin, Timofeev, Paramonov, & Balandin, 2015; Balandina, Balandin, Koucheryavy, & Mouromtsev, 2015; Korzun & Balandin, 2016). As a simplified ecosystem development scenario, we can consider the following example. A number of solutions exists that enables joint use of various sets of devices by controlling them via centralized management system in a cloud. The problem, however, is that such a solution implies high scalability restrictions. The user becomes strongly dependent on a managing service in a cloud, which is physically located somewhere, possible on another side of the planet. This problem creates a lot of issues and challenges, starting from additional delays due to distant data transmission and queuing before getting service in cloud, to the questions of privacy. Just by cutting the outgoing Internet connections the user will completely lost service. The strangest of all is that the devices that are to deliver required services are still around the user. They have capabilities and resources to provide the services that the user needs.

Another important observation is that most of modern devices have significant embedded memory, processing power and communication capabilities, including support of short range communications, e.g., via Bluetooth. Some devices have advanced embedded control and management system, which could perform various tasks beyond basic functional of the device. Moreover, for the most time we see that the device resources are significantly underused. As a result, we for most of devices there is significant resource redundancy.

This fact gives us an opportunity to revise the basic principle of how services are organized and delivered to the users. It is common practice for Internet services that instead of placing all service components to the same physical device, services are implemented in a distributed manner with the involvement of multiple devices.

The similar principle at the device level recently become more known under name fog computing. But in fact, this principle has been proposed many times in the past under various names. In this book, we are going to use term non-centralized smart spaces, or just Smart Spaces. We particularly focus on Smart Spaces architecture that delivers new kinds of smart services by directly utilizing processing and storage capabilities of the surrounding devices. A central role in this architecture is given to the personal mobile device, e.g., smartphone or tablet. The personal mobile device keeps track of personal preferences and is the main orchestrating unit of the Smart Space.

## BACKGROUND

The volume and complexity of information and services in the Internet is growing so fast that absolute majority of users cannot efficiently utilize the existing multitude of services, and even are not aware of the existing possibilities. A number of ideas and technologies have been proposed recently for making pervasive and mobile services intelligent and sensitive to the actual users' needs (Cook, Augusto, & Jakkula, 2009; Kjeldskov, Skov, Nielsen, Thorup, & Vestergaard, 2013). The target key features are:

1.  Interoperability support for devices, services, and users localized in a physical environment,
2.  Personalized proactive behavior and coordination models for applications.

The low level of interoperability and communication between services results in high fragmentation, i.e., information collected in one service is rarely accessible in another. The key challenge is intelligent use of maximum collected information by as many as possible applications that potentially can benefit of the information. In this case, service provision chains become lengthy and necessitate involvement of a multitude of surrounding embedded and consumer electronics devices, and especially personal devices that accompanies the user most of time. There is a demand of a framework architecture that enables to combine multitude of services and devices in order to create personalized and context-aware service experience, including proactive delivery.

Book (Cook & Das, 2004) gives the following definition of Smart Spaces: "Smart Space is able to acquire and apply knowledge about its environment and to adapt to its inhabitants in order to improve their experience in that environment". This definition assumes continues interaction of a user with the surrounding environment that is targeted in continuous adaptation of services to current needs of the user. This interaction is enabled by:

- **Sensing Functionality:** For gathering information about the space and the user.
- **Adaptation Functionality:** For reacting to the detected changes.
- **Effecting Functionality:** For changing the surrounding space to benefit the user.

Based on the definition the main focus of Smart Spaces is on user and the idea to apply principle of space-based computing for delivering enhanced services (see more details in Chapter 2 further). Idea is that common information is shared in a space for joint access. The basic operational element is a smart computational object (or agent). Agents can reason knowledge and make decisions using this information and in accordance with the application goals. The parallel processes in the space cooperating via their agents that publishing/retrieving data into/from the space. This asynchronous publish-based communication model defines a system as a composition of autonomous agents running in parallel and interacting by sharing information. In IoT environments, personal mobile devices (e.g., smartphone, tablet) and embedded devices (e.g., sensors, consumer electronics) become "first-class devices" for hosting such agents, along with traditional desktop and server computers.

The smart spaces paradigm inherits the models of space-based computing and provides a conceptual way for creating smart environments in IoT environments as proposed by (Korzun, Balandin, & Gurtov, 2013). In the last decade, smart spaces have grown from a sub-stream of ubiquitous computing in to a self-contained paradigm. The paradigm aims at development of ubiquitous computing environment, where participating smart objects acquire and apply knowledge to adapt services to the inhabitants in order to enhance user experience, quality and reliability of the provided information as illustrated in (Balandin & Waris, 2009). The target is information components of a smart environment and their effective conjunction with communication and decision components.

In contrasted to the IoT definition, a smart object is not strictly associated with a particular host device and less focused on the underlying network communication means. Compared to the generic definition from multi-agent systems, a smart object can

1.  Identify itself as a part of the environment and application,
2.  Understand their state,
3.  Operate with a certain part of the shared content,
4.  Make over this part own interpretations, decisions, and actions.

A smart object is an autonomous information processing unit. Consequently, each smart object is represented as a programmed computational process, which is responsible for a distinguishable portion of the application logic and hosted on one or more devices of the environment. Smart objects are not attached to a particular device, as any available device can host the object. Services are constructed as interaction of smart objects in a shared space. The smart space can be deployed in a cloud or on user's devices that interact with each other and use pertinent services regardless of the physical location. In this book we use the term "agent" instead of "smart object" to emphasize that it is a program executed on some devices.

The Smart Space can be seen as a kind of service cocoon that surrounds the user and relocates together with the user. It is especially important to note that at the same time the user is surrounded by multiple Smart Space cocoons. Each Smart Space has own clearly focused mission. The Smart Spaces can overlap, which in practice means that they include the same services, use same physical devices and share some information. The general view of the Smart Spaces hierarchy logic is illustrated by Figure 1.

From the system point of view, a smart space provides an infrastructure (a smart environment) for interaction of smart objects on a common knowledge base, i.e., mechanisms for reasoning and decision-making are provided, in addition to basic information sharing and network communication. Typically, such an infrastructure covers a spatially restricted area equipped with IoT devices and access to global networks and the Internet, thus possibly communicating with other smart spaces. Each space is uniquely named and addressable. When a user appears in the physical area her devices and agents join the smart space using the infrastructure.

*Figure 1. Hierarchical layers of smart spaces with the user in the center*

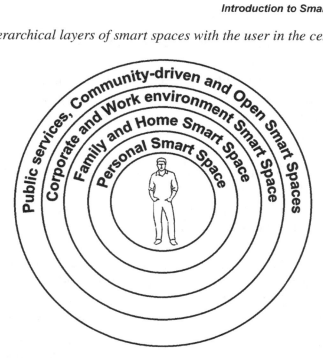

The key concepts for Smart Spaces are mobility, distribution and context awareness. These are addressed by the recent advances in wireless networking technologies as well as processing and storage capabilities, which have moved mobile and consumer electronics devices beyond their traditional areas of applications and allow their use for a broader scope of services. The significant computing power and high-speed data connections of the modern mobile devices allow them to become information processing and communication hubs that perform rather complex computations locally and distribute the results. This lets multiple devices interact with each other and form ad-hoc dynamic, distributed computation platforms. Together, they form a space where via a number of wireless technologies the users can access a huge variety of services. Similarly, existing and future services form spaces that cater for a variety of needs ranging from browsing to interactive video conversations. These services surround the user all the time and have access to large amounts of data. Over time they can learn users' needs and personal preferences, making it possible to build even more advanced services that proactively predict those needs and propose valuable services in the given environment before the users realize it themselves. These layers, each of which can utilize a number of technologies form a smart environment, which is called the Smart Space. Another important aspect is that Smart Spaces improve the interaction between users and their physical environments, allowing more efficient consumption of available resources such as energy.

The smart space is taking into account environmental conditions described as a context, plus predefined and collected information on requirements of the user and smart space nodes (stored in their profiles). This feature of the smart spaces has key role to achieve high degree of responsiveness and managing systems adaptively to the dynamic changes of the environment. The general reference model of the profile-based context-aware smart space is proposed in (Smirnov, Kashevnik, Shilov, Boldyrev, Balandin, & Oliver, 2009), as Figure 2 illustrates.

Each node can be located at several physical devices or several nodes can be located at one physical device. A node can access a predefined limited set of information storages to acquire information units from them. The nodes exchange information units / fragments, which are stored in the distributed storage accessible by the nodes of the smart space. The ontology defines possible capabilities of the nodes in the smart space and sets some constraints on these capabilities in the form of user interfaces (IUs) and information fragments, which are stored in the information storages.

The information storages can be physically located at one or several physical devices or several information storages can be located at one physical device. IUs can be transferred between information storages in order to become accessible to appropriate nodes. To estimate the efficiency of the information allocation the cost function has been introduced. The "cost" of IU transfer can be calculated as a sum of IU transmission and IU receiving

*Figure 2. Reference model of the information recycling-enabled smart space*

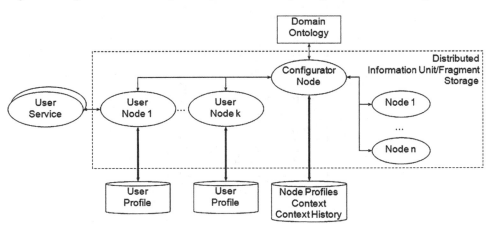

costs. These costs are different for different information storages. However, cost of IU transmission from the given information storage is constant and does not depend on the destination information storage. Analogously, the cost of IU receiving for a given information storage is constant and does not depend on the transmitting information storage.

To increase the efficiency of the smart space operation the personification is required. For this purpose, the users and devices have to be described by a set of characteristics required for interaction with other nodes.

User nodes communicate with user profiles. The structure of the user profile is illustrated by Figure 3. The user profiles are stored in information storages accessible by user nodes and contain the following information:

- User identification and auxiliary information, e.g., user ID, name, personal data, contact information such as e-mail, mobile phone.
- User privacy policies, e.g., calendar can be shared with the certain configurator nodes, phonebook cannot be shared.
- User preferences defined as the rules of the user preferred behavior, e.g., microphone loudness, light brightness. Models and algorithms for detection of the user preferences are out of the scope of this book.

The node profile is served for setting communications with other nodes. The node profile example is shown in Figure 4. The node profile is stored in the information storage accessible by the configurator node and contains the following information.

*Figure 3. User profile*

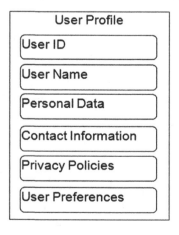

*Figure 4. Node profile*

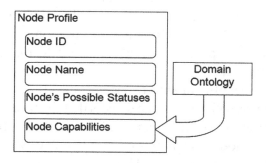

- Node identification (its ID and name).
- Possible statuses of the node (e.g., light is on, 30% brightness).
- Node capabilities (what the node can do) - described in the domain ontology.

The context describes current environmental status of the smart space. It is represented by the set of statuses of nodes constituting the smart space. The context forms a part of the information environment where the nodes interact as discussed in (Brezillon, 1999). The urgency of the information contained in the context can be defined in relation to all nodes taking part in information exchange. In course of time the context changes, thus a new context appears. The context history stores these contexts. The history of contexts enables:

- Information recycling (in what conditions an information unit/fragment was actual),
- Finding behavior patterns for users (user preferences),
- Finding behavior patterns for nodes (anticipation of node statuses).

The user nodes can interact with nodes that represent other applications. For example, a node of the application responsible for user's activities planner regularly interacts with the calendar node to get information about current and future user's appointments. In practice, such cooperation is implemented as exchange of information between agents that implement the corresponding applications. For exchanging information and statuses the agents use asynchronous data exchange via the shared field in the smart service database. For example, by having access to current smart space context the calendar can generate information unit that the user is going to have a presentation in the room, where he/she is now. This signal/flag is interpreted by another node responsible for arranging presentation. When the time comes, the user will not need to waste time on uploading presentation and negotiating other practicalities. All these processes could be well formalized and handled automatically by the smart space.

One of the main benefits of smart spaces comes from situations when an agent that represents service or device detects that the user entered to the area with the new smart space. As was mentioned before, the key property provided by the Smart Spaces nodes (agents) is interoperability, which facilitates their participation in new smart spaces. This is especially important when we think about new opportunities that are delivered in IoT-enabled world. In particular, in IoT environments the smart space shall provide the following interoperability properties.

- IoT environment is enhanced by applying shared view of available resources and services.
- Better user experience is achieved by easy integration of new devices into the IoT environment and by seamless access of information distributed over the multi-device system from any of the devices as discussed in (Balandin, Bjorksten, Hakkila, Jekkonen, Makela, & Roimela, 2007).
- Storage, retrieval, reasoning, and decision-making over this multi-source heterogeneous information are supported by knowledge base infrastructure deployed in the IoT environment.

A smart application provides its users with services using the best available resources for all kinds of surrounding and personal devices that the users can exploit in the environment. The interoperability properties allow constructing applications where the notion of service emerges from activities and capabilities of the participating agents on end-user and environment devices. The reasoning mechanisms are based on enhanced methods of deductive closure and allow continuously defining new relations and logical links between all information elements in the knowledge base. The user can access services from any device that is able to host the corresponding user interface agents.

Within each smart space the information is organized according to its owners. The agents run on personal and surrounding devices, sharing user-related and environmental information, i.e., forming information content $A$. The corpus $R(A)$ continuously performs data mining operations on the shared content as was presented by Boldyrev at el. (2009). Hidden knowledge is extracted and the information is transformed into interconnected knowledge. Corpus $R(A)$ is delivered by local reasoning and deductive closure algorithms. Altogether, agents create the knowledge-driven functionally of the application, as illustrated in Figure 5 for user "Alice".

Typically, a smart space represents one area of user's life, e.g., work environment, home environment, healthcare environment. The user can interact with a number of spaces, as shown in Figure 6. Smart spaces are dynamic, and all the time the content must be synchronized driven by the user applications needs. This way the applications are making exchange of relevant knowledge between spaces that belongs to the same or different owners (users, areas, or applications). Split and merge operations applied not only to user's information (e.g., A, B, C, and D in Figure 3), but also to corpuses (e.g., R(A), R(B), R(C), and R(D), resp.).

In this scenario, Alice can decide to break and reconfigure her current spaces into many smaller spaces. This may be made in any manner including removing all information and creating multiple individual smaller or even empty spaces to making complete copies of the current space.

The above provided overview allows us to conclude that the Smart Spaces architecture provides reach functionality and good flexibility that are sufficient for development advanced services. It is clear that the Smart Spaces concept is an opportunity for consumer electronics and service industries to get closer to the users, proactively assist them, and as a result optimize the consumption of critical resources. In order to guarantee broad adoption and success of

*Figure 5. Example of Alice's smart space: her personal agents cooperatively create the services*

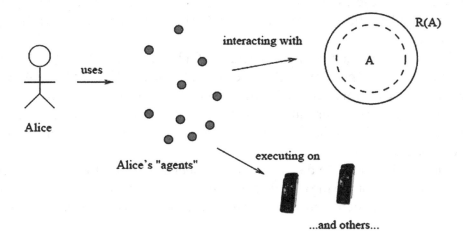

*Figure 6. Multiple space interaction: merge and split process are driven by the applications needs*

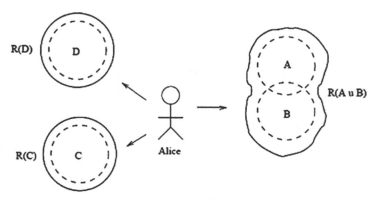

Smart Spaces architecture in practice both efficient communication and service development frameworks have to be proposed.

Another important observation is that it is natural for mobile devices to become the personalized access point. Mobile devices are the closest gadgets to the users so it is logical to see them as the primary user interface to the Smart Space. Plus, modern personal mobile devices, e.g., smartphones and tablets have significant processing and storage capabilities, so even significant part of Smart Spaces processing can be handled directly by such devices.

For example, the management functionality should inform the Smart Space about the user preferences and see how to obtain the favorite service of the user from the modules available in the given space. By having access to a large amount of personal information (e.g. calendar, email, etc.) and being carried by the user, the device can learn about the individual preferences and thus find or build up new services and offer them to the user at the most convenient time.

The R&D community is well capable of addressing functional and non-functional product properties. However, for solutions intended to be deployed commercially as Smart Space products, there are additional properties that we encourage researchers and developers to take into account already at an early phase in order to increase the probability that their results will end up in the market.

Later in the book, we discuss the key properties related to the efficiency of product creation; to the usability of arbitrary Smart Spaces in the physical space; and to their deployment as commercial products. Within each category, we discuss a set of key properties and present a list of simple questions that allow developers to subjectively estimate how easy it would be to make the leap from a technical Smart Space solution to a sustainable product desired by users and valuable to businesses. We do not expect that the questions would be answered in the affirmative in all or even most of the categories for any prospective Smart Space. However, if any of the categories scores poorly in any of the categories it should prompt the developer to reconsider the assumptions of the R&D effort. Finally, the questions can be translated into taxonomy and used for classifying Smart Space concepts and implementations.

## INTRODUCTION TO THE RELATED CORE TECHNOLOGIES

Development of Internet of Things infrastructure and exponential growth of a number and variety of sensors are closely linked to the development of Smart Spaces technologies. It is due to the fact that these technologies are the main sources of the context data and information describing the physical world and mapping it into the virtual space. Development of the sensors ecosystem enables continuous monitoring of characteristics of any physical space. As a consequence, is allows taking proactive actions to direct environment conditions in a desired direction. As a result, we can automate many services that currently require overprovision of resources or human intervention. Thus, success of the Smart Spaces services depends on how efficiently it will use IoT infrastructure and sensor networks.

A service-oriented IoT-aware application can be constructed as a distributed multi-agent system hosted on a multitude of devices. A smart application acquires knowledge about the environment and its human users and applies the knowledge to improve service consumption and user experience.

The IoT paradigm grew from ubiquitous computing and now evolves to the architectural model of loosely coupled decentralized system of objects augmented with sensing/actuation, processing, and network capabilities - from everyday things in embedded digital equipment and consumer electronics to the existing Internet and Web. Physical and digital entities are transformed into smart objects. Each smart object acts on its own and keeps a part of the application logic, e.g., senses the local environment and the world, communicates with other objects, and interacts with users. The IoT technology provides a ubiquitous networked environment - IoT environment, where diverse devices can communicate using various means of wired and wireless connectivity.

The smartness (or intelligence) property of IoT objects supports forming a smart environment in a given IoT environment and its configuration of physical entities. Human users receive services based on cooperative activity of smart objects in acquiring and applying knowledge about the environment and the users. Typical components of a smart environment are shown in Figure 7 (left side), following the discussion in (Augusto, Callaghan, Cook, Kameas, & Satoh, 2013).

Operations in a smart environment can be viewed as the following cycle as presented in (Bartolini, Milosevic, D'Elia, Farella, Benini, & Cinotti, 2012):

1. Perceiving the state of the environment,
2. Reasoning about the state together with service application goals and outcomes of possible actions,
3. Acting upon the environment to change the state.

Further in the book we are focused on models and technologies of space-based computing for construction of information components. They, in turn, feed decision-making components with appropriate knowledge for methods of ambient intelligence as discussed in (Kiljander, Takalo-Mattila, Etelapera, Soininen, & Keinanen, 2011; Mayer, Verborgh, Kovatsch, & Mattern, 2016).

Another source of enormous volume of information is the World Wide Web. It is especially important when there is a need for interpretation of the obtained information, access to generic data and so on. From this respect the main enabler for Smart Spaces is the semantic web and its underlying technologies, such as Resource Description Framework (RDF) as discussed in (Oliver, 2008; Horrocks, 2008; Gutierrez, Hurtado, Mendelzon, & Pérez,

*Figure 7. The layered structure of components in a smart environment (left); source areas for related models and technologies (right)*

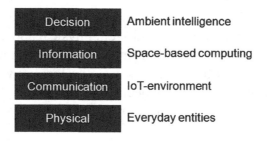

2011; Martín-Recuerda, 2005). The Semantic Web technology provides information representation, including structure and semantics, in a machine-readable form. The Semantic Web is an enabler for creating a true web of information and opens the door for the creation of sophisticated Smart Space services where most of the informational interactions happen in an automatic fashion. It completely changes the nature of applications from the current monolithic to highly distributed, mobile and agent-like entities.

Devices need to act as information processing and storage units and the resulting services need to be delivered to the consumers. The mobile device, due to being available to users and possessing significant internal processing power and data storage, should be a central component of the personal Smart Spaces. For interaction between the mobile device and the smart objects surrounding it, the most efficient approach seems to be the expansion of intra-device connectivity solutions.

Unfortunately, there is today no existing optimized interface in the mobile industry similar to ISA, USB, PCI or PCI Express available in the PC world. This has strong historical reasons, especially the need to optimize device performance as much as possible. As a consequence, a large number of sometimes incompatible interface alternatives exist for connecting purpose specific components, and strongly monolithic mobile device architectures include extension busses such as I2C and SPI, which provide a bandwidth of at most a few Mbit/s. The current situation contradicts the target of easy expansion outside of the device and could be seen as one of the blocking factors for next round of progress in development of mobile device enabled Smart Spaces.

Finally, as we mentioned before, the space-based computing has roots in communication models of parallel and distributed programming as discussed in (Nixon, Simperl, Krummenacher, & Martin-Recuerda, 2008), so formally let us include those models to the list of core technologies.

# THE MAIN POINTS FOR CONSIDERATION BY SMART SPACES DEVELOPERS

As discussed before, the key technical enablers for the broad adoption of smart spaces paradigm are mostly in place. Therefore, we claim that now is the right time to start development of smart spaces applications and services. But before diving into technical details, which are addressed in the following Chapters, we still want to discuss key non-technical issues related to development of Smart Spaces. By talking about non-technical properties, we primarily address challenges related to usability and commercial deployment. Some solutions for these problems can be found in the technical plane, but they should be considered at the early stage of system design. Based on our experience we feel that it would be beneficial for the R&D community to stop on these points because despite their importance for the final result, these issues are typically ignored in the beginning and become visible only at the later phases of development process.

The product properties of Smart Space systems can be split into two categories. Functional properties are dependent on the functionality that the Smart Space should offer to its users. These properties are too dependent on the use scenarios and the corresponding analysis is provided in Chapter 5. Later in this section we assume that Smart Spaces can be used to provide arbitrary functionality and therefore the desired composition of these properties varies case by case. The R&D community is already adequately addressing non-functional properties such as resource awareness and security, which may be difficult and expensive to incorporate into the solution once the product is ready.

There are further technical properties that are not related to any particular Smart Space as a single product, but rather to the efficiency of the process that creates them as a group or category of products. The following elaborates on these in more detail and presents questions that can be used to estimate how well a work-in-progress Smart Space can be productized. For each category, we formulate five most relevant questions to be considered.

Interoperability of the devices and services in the Smart Space is critical since Smart Spaces are unlikely to comply with a single particular architecture as discussed in (Ovaska, Cinotti, & Toninelli, 2012). For a specific Smart Space, it is possible to create a successful stand-alone system that fulfills its business objectives. However, in the absence of adequate interoperability mechanisms the Smart Space will not be able to achieve economies-of-scale and ecosystem benefits that come from cost efficient mass production and ability to maximize the value add of investments through specialization and reuse. Questions:

1. Is the Smart Space composed of components that interoperate using a clear set of common interfaces (low integration effort of planned system)?

2.   Is the Smart Space providing an interoperability mechanism for non-predefined components (low integration effort for extensions or enhancements)?
3.   Is the Smart Space constructed from components that can be re-used in other Smart Spaces (lower risk for invested effort, support for evolution)?
4.   Is the Smart Space allowing all components to be implemented using any technical solutions (low adaptation effort by developers and businesses)?
5.   Is the Smart Space composition implementable using easily available and well known development methodology and tools (efficient development effort)?

If you get all "yes" answers then your solution has high interoperability. But if majority of answers is "no" then there is significant space for interoperability improvement, i.e., more standard solutions should be adopted to lower the development costs.

Smart spaces are inherently versatile as unique combinations of devices and services serving some purposes in a particular context. The nature of Smart Spaces as systems deployed in a physical space also make it more expensive to upgrade them in a managed fashion as time goes by. It is important to be able to easily extend the functionality of the Smart Space as it emerges over time.

Questions:

1.   Is the Smart Space providing access to Internet functionality as de-facto standards?
2.   Is the Smart Space based on popular device platforms and Internet solutions?
3.   Is the Smart Space supporting the addition and modification of components?
4.   Is the Smart Space applicable to components with a wide performance range?
5.   Is the Smart Space supporting use of functionality from a different Smart Space?

If you get all "yes" then your solution has good extensibility. But if majority of answers is "no" then extensibility of your solution shall be improved, i.e., the later enhancements should be supported, or access to complementary or additional functionality provided.

The complexity of developing and operating the Smart Space determines how easily many other properties can be improved. Logical complexity increases the risk involved in starting to develop it as a product, whereas implementation complexity reduces efficiency of installation, maintenance and upgrading.

Questions:

1.   Is the Smart Space logically coherent and simple for an average developer?
2.   Is the Smart Space installable and maintainable cost efficiently by a non-expert?
3.   Is the Smart Space following a logical classification, supporting marketing efforts?
4.   Is the Smart Space adhering to a governance model to manage features and IPR?
5.   Is the Smart Space available in verified configurations, for distribution channels?

If you get all "yes" then your solution is simple to develop and operate. But if majority of answers is "no" then complexity of developing and operating of your solution shall be improved, i.e., the development and operation should be made easier.

For the adoption of Smart Spaces, it is crucial to go beyond the technology enabler development, demonstrators and small trials. Smart spaces must address real and everyday consumer needs in a way that generates demand for the technical solutions. In particular, their accessibility needs to be targeted to suit the intended users of the various Smart Spaces, and the Smart Space must promise enough commercial added value compared to the costs involved.

We are presenting a set of further questions that can be used subjectively to estimate how a Smart Space addresses some key properties. If some property is addressed particularly weakly, the researcher or developer may want to determine whether that is intentional or whether to focus available resources to improve that.

The first property to focus on is the generality or specificity of intended users, because the brief first impression must convince the intended user of the value that the Smart Space can provide, and being attractive to more potential users will increase the chances that more will become users.

Questions:

1.   Can the expected user be from any age group (flexibility and reception of novelty)?

2.    Can the expected user be of any occupation or life situation (habits, social needs)?
3.    Can the Smart Space be used with any level of attention (effort/means to interact)?
4.    Can the Smart Space be used with any level of technical skill?
5.    Can the Smart Space be used regardless of the level of mental or physical abilities?

If you get all "yes" such solutions are intended for very generic user and thus has potentially large user base, so the overall scale of adoption is primary determined by the rest of the properties. But if majority of answers is "no" then the solution targets very specific user type, other circumstances (e.g. location) need to make it likely that such users would be available in sufficient numbers to make meaningful development of such solution.

The next challenge is to make the users aware of the existence of the Smart Space, which may be something very purpose specific in a particular physical space, composed of arbitrary physical elements that are not obvious indicators to any user that there would be a Smart Space in the area.

Questions:

1.    Is the Smart Space associated with a concrete, visible object (position/coverage)?
2.    Is the Smart Space associated with a recognizable or familiar object or person?
3.    Is the Smart Space prominently labeled or indicated (sensory perception)?
4.    Is the Smart Space in a physically and information-wise uncluttered area?
5.    Is the Smart Space in a context occurring frequently with other similar spaces (possibility to extrapolate or interpolate, or to memorize for re-use)?

If you get all "yes" then your solution is easy to find and connect to. But if majority of answers is "no" then the solution is difficult to find so there is risk that it will be invisible. It is recommend carefully considering how to promote the existence and availability of your applications in the environment, or communicated via some other means such as advertisements or trainings, until a sufficient level of awareness has been established among the intended user base.

Users can be aware of the availability of the Smart Space, but were not involved in its preparation and do not know that it would offer potentially attractive services or value. There is no general means to make all users understand the value of all potential Smart Spaces a priori, but functional familiarity with their representations may be possible.

Questions:

1. Is the Smart Space serving a similar purpose as an associated object (extrapolate)?
2. Is the Smart Space used in similar ways by different users (examples)?
3. Is the Smart Space performing in a similar range as the associated object?
4. Is the Smart Space starting from a common user need in the context (motivation)?
5. Is the Smart Space involved in the daily habits of its users (likelihood of learning)?

If you get all "yes" then your solution is easy to comprehend. But if majority of answers is "no" then likely your solution is hard to comprehend, so the contents and value proposition should be communicated via some other means such as instructions. Another way is to simplify it or split functionality to a number of applications so that the functionality is comprehensible in expected usage situations.

When the users start to interact with a newly encountered unique Smart Space available in a particular location, it may be their only occasion to use the system. It is important to serve the intended users by adapting to the interaction types that suit them best in the given circumstances.

Questions:

1. Is the Smart Space usable with any modality (ability to serve users at their terms)?
2. Is the Smart Space usable by interacting with a concrete object (interaction learning effort)?
3. Is the Smart Space usable as an extension of existing object functionality (low cognitive learning effort)?
4. Is the Smart Space usable with different methods leading to a function (ability to serve different user logics and approaches)?
5. Is the Smart Space usable with a similar effort regardless of the level of expertise (ability to serve users of various capabilities)?

If you get all "yes" then your solution supports intuitive interaction interface. But if majority of answers is "no" then interaction requires meticulous effort and should be made easier through more alternatives suiting various user groups. Alternatively you could think of better integration with objects existing in the space or in the user's possession.

User interactions with a unique Smart Space can never fully satisfy the needs of all intended users: Better adaptation to the individual user's imported configurations and preferences can compensate for the limitations.

Questions:

1.  Does the Smart Space provide parameters to configure most of its functionality?
2.  Does the Smart Space identify the parameters unambiguously for portability?
3.  Is the Smart Space linked with user accessible example configurations (ability to learn how to adapt the system)?
4.  Is the Smart Space capable of exporting and importing configurations (ability to automatically apply selected configurations)?
5.  Is the Smart Space capable of applying partially fitting configurations (portability of settings across similar but different systems)?

If you get all "yes" then the user specific preferences can be intuitively applied. But if majority of answers is "no" then tailoring requires meticulous effort and should be made easier by adopting preference descriptions commonly used by comparable users and services.

The final condition for a successful Smart Space is commercial viability. There needs to be a balance between the investments on deployment and operating costs and the expected income for all stakeholders. Attempting to estimate these may feel useless, but may also help in adjusting the ambition levels of the development effort.

Questions:

1.  Is the Smart Space fully sponsored by any of multiple committed business parties?
2.  Is the Smart Space making the contributions of stakeholders visible to their potential clients (support for advertisement funded business model)?
3.  Is the Smart Space operation clearly profitable after potential costs?

4.  Is the Smart Space composed of elements that are fully reusable in other spaces (ability to recoup investments in case of lifetime expiration or failure)?
5.  Is the Smart Space managing the rights of all stakeholders investing in it (reduce business risk over the lifetime of the system)?

If you get all "yes" then you have low business risk. But if majority of answers is "no" then business risks are high and the ambitions of the R&D effort should be considered accordingly.

The attractiveness must also be made known to developers and users: what it can provide them, how well it does that, and how it can be used subsequently.

Questions:

1.  Is the Smart Space suggesting potentially useful non-requested functionality (value beyond expectations)?
2.  Is the Smart Space capable of recognizing user's interest in similar spaces (ability to speed up adoption and distribution through network effect)?
3.  Is the Smart Space detecting and repeating successful usage patterns (automation)?
4.  Is the Smart Space detecting and correcting unsuccessful usage patterns?
5.  Is the Smart Space conveying an image of continuity backed up by credible sponsors (trust that it is worth the personal resources invested in using it)?

If you get all "yes" then further use of the deployed technologies and solutions is encouraged. But if majority of answers is "no" then further use beyond the immediate reason that the user started to interact is discouraged, and any economies-of-scale benefits are difficult to obtain.

Finally, for the Smart Spaces to become successful as a broad category of systems available in physical locations, it is important to support a healthy ecosystem of multiple actors with versatile development capabilities and business interests.

Questions:

1.  Is the Smart Space possible to deploy in multiple combinations (ability to incorporate elements from multiple vendors)?

2.  Is the Smart Space possible to deploy at multiple levels of quality (ability to adapt and apply the space in multiple environments)?
3.  Is the Smart Space exempt from regulatory or other non-user imposed constraints (reliability of available functionality)?
4.  Is the Smart Space capable of self-configuration to accommodate enhancements?
5.  Is the Smart Space offering a light-weight licensing for enhancements?

If you get all "yes" then the freedom of building additional or complementary business using the Smart Space is unconstrained. But if majority of answers is "no" then the Smart Space constrains external innovations, and any ecosystem benefits are difficult to obtain.

The above summarizes our vision of the additional properties that we encourage researchers and developers to take into account already at an early phase in order to increase the probability that their results will end up in the market. We do not pretend that the provide list of questions is correct for all situations and exceptions are possible. But we hope these questions help you in designing your Smart Spaces solutions.

## CONCLUSION

The chapter is opening the main discussion addressed by the book: how Smart Spaces can be broadly adopted for use in their everyday lives, by paying attention to pragmatic product issues. The chapter gives an introduction to smart environments and the Smart Spaces paradigm. We present the general concept and underlying technologies. We discuss the existing technologies that might play the key role in future development of Smart Spaces. An important observation is that both efficient communication and service development frameworks have to be proposed and widely accepted in order to guarantee the broad success of Smart Spaces.

Nowadays it is getting clear that the Smart Spaces paradigm provides great opportunity for the new spin in consumer electronics and services industries. It allows services to come even closer to the users, better understand real-time demands and proactively help user to get desired services. As a result, one can expect significant increase of the user satisfaction and along with optimization of consumption of critical resources.

The chapter provides general overview of the main related technologies. A number of supporting technologies are listed. For example, it is discussed that although the low-level communication IoT technologies are becoming more and more effective, the higher levels for embedding intelligence into IoT environments still need elaboration, making the wide area of high research and development interest. We discuss properties of the Smart Spaces design related to:

- Efficiency of product creation,
- Usability of arbitrary Smart Spaces in the physical space,
- To their deployment as commercial products.

Within each of these categories we have proposed a set of key properties and presented a list of five simple questions. These questions shall allow the developers to subjectively estimate how easy it would be to make the leap from a technical Smart Space solution to a sustainable product desired by users and valuable for business. We do not expect that the questions would be answered in the affirmative in all or even most of the categories for any prospective Smart Space. However, if a solution gets low score in any of the categories it should prompt the developer to reconsider the assumptions of the planned research, development and deployment efforts. Finally, the questions can be translated into taxonomy and used for classifying Smart Space concepts and implementations.

# REFERENCES

Augusto, J. C., Callaghan, V., Cook, D., Kameas, A., & Satoh, I. (2013). Intelligent Environments: A manifesto. *Human-centric Computing and Information Sciences*, *3*(12), 1–18.

Balandin, S., Bjorksten, M., Hakkila, J., Jekkonen, J., Makela, K., & Roimela, K. (2007). Supporting the notion of seamlessness in personal content management. *Proceedings of the Second IASTED International Conference on Human Computer Interaction* (pp. 250-256). ACTA Press.

Balandin, S., & Waris, H. (2009). Key Properties in the Development of Smart Spaces. *Proceedings of International Conference on Universal Access in Human-Computer Interaction. Intelligent and Ubiquitous Interaction Environments, LNCS* (Vol. 5615, pp. 3-12). Springer. doi:10.1007/978-3-642-02710-9_1

Balandina, E., Balandin, S., Koucheryavy, Y., & Mouromtsev, D. (2015). IoT Use Cases in Healthcare and Tourism. *Proceedings of IEEE 17th Conference on Business Informatics* (pp. 37-44). IEEE. doi:10.1109/CBI.2015.16

Bartolini, S., Milosevic, B., DElia, A., Farella, E., Benini, L., & Cinotti, T. S. (2012). Reconfigurable natural interaction in smart environments. *Personal and Ubiquitous Computing, 16*(7), 943–956. doi:10.1007/s00779-011-0454-5

Brezillon, P. (1999). Context in Problem Solving: A Survey. *The Knowledge Engineering Review, 14*(1), 47–80. doi:10.1017/S0269888999141018

Cook, D., Augusto, J., & Jakkula, V. (2009). Ambient intelligence: Technologies, applications, and opportunities. *Pervasive and Mobile Computing, 5*(4), 277–298. doi:10.1016/j.pmcj.2009.04.001

Cook, D., & Das, S. K. (2004). *Smart environments: Technology, protocols and applications.* John Wiley & Sons. doi:10.1002/047168659X

Gutierrez, C., Hurtado, C. A., Mendelzon, A. O., & Pérez, J. (2011). Foundations of Semantic Web Databases. *Journal of Computer and System Sciences, 77*(3), 520–541. doi:10.1016/j.jcss.2010.04.009

Horrocks, I. (2008). Ontologies and the Semantic Web. *Communications of the ACM, 51*(12), 58–67. doi:10.1145/1409360.1409377

Kiljander, J., Takalo-Mattila, J., Etelapera, M., Soininen, J.-P., & Keinanen, K. (2011). Enabling End-Users to Configure Smart Environments. *Proceedings of 2011 IEEE/IPSJ 11th International Symposium on Applications and the Internet* (pp. 303-308). IEEE. doi:10.1109/SAINT.2011.58

Kjeldskov, J., Skov, M., Nielsen, G., Thorup, S., & Vestergaard, M. (2013). Digital urban ambience: Mediating context on mobile devices in a city. *Pervasive and Mobile Computing, 9*(5), 738–749. doi:10.1016/j.pmcj.2012.05.002

Korzun, D., & Balandin, S. (2016). Personalizing the Internet of Things Using Mobile Information Services. *Proceedings of The Tenth International Conference on Mobile Ubiquitous Computing, Systems, Services and Technologies* (pp. 184-189). IARIA.

Korzun, D., Balandin, S., & Gurtov, A. (2013). Deployment of Smart Spaces in Internet of Things: Overview of the Design Challenges. *Proceedings of Internet of Things, Smart Spaces, and Next Generation Networks and Systems: 13th International Conference NEW2AN 2013 and 5th Conference ruSMART 2013, LNCS* (Vol. 8121, pp. 48-59). Springer.

Korzun, D. G., Borodin, A. V., Timofeev, I. A., Paramonov, I. V., & Balandin, S. I. (2015). Digital Assistance Services for Emergency Situations in Personalized Mobile Healthcare: Smart Space Based Approach. *Proceedings of International Conference on Biomedical Engineering and Computational Technologies* (pp. 62-67). IEEE. doi:10.1109/SIBIRCON.2015.7361852

Martín-Recuerda, F. (2005). Towards Cspaces: A new perspective for the Semantic Web. *Proceedings of 1st IFIP WG12.5 Working Conference of Industrial Applications of Semantic Web* (Vol. 188, pp. 113-139). Springer. doi:10.1007/0-387-29248-9_7

Mayer, S., Verborgh, R., Kovatsch, M., & Mattern, F. (2016). Smart Configuration of Smart Environments. *IEEE Transactions on Automation Science and Engineering, 13*(3), 1247–1255. doi:10.1109/TASE.2016.2533321

Nixon, L. J. B., Simperl, E., Krummenacher, R., & Martin-Recuerda, F. (2008). Tuplespace-based Computing for the Semantic Web: A Survey of the State-of-the-Art. *The Knowledge Engineering Review, 23*(2), 181–212. doi:10.1017/S0269888907001221

Oliver, I. (2008). Towards the Dynamic Semantic Web. *Proceedings of Internet of Things, Smart Spaces, and Next Generation Networking: 8th International Conference NEW2AN 2008 and 1st Conference ruSMART 2008, LNCS* (Vol. 5174, pp. 258-259). Springer. doi:10.1007/978-3-540-85500-2_23

Ovaska, E., Cinotti, T. S., & Toninelli, A. (2012). The Design Principles and Practices of Interoperable Smart Spaces. In X. Liu & Y. Li (Eds.), *Advanced Design Approaches to Emerging Software Systems: Principles, Methodologies and Tools* (pp. 18–47). IGI Global. doi:10.4018/978-1-60960-735-7.ch002

Smirnov, A., Kashevnik, A., Shilov, N., Boldyrev, S., Balandin, S., & Oliver, I. (2009). Context-Aware Smart Space - Reference Model. *Proceedings of International Conference on Advanced Information Networking and Applications Workshops* (pp. 261-265). IEEE. doi:10.1109/WAINA.2009.104

## KEY TERMS AND DEFINITIONS

**Agent:** A software module that represents simplest version of node in the smart space. An agent can reason knowledge and make decisions using this information and in accordance with the application goals.

**Behavior Rule:** Behavior rules are defined for nodes in the following format: "if {information unit} then {action}."

**Configurator Node:** This node manages (accumulates and provides access to) information about other participating nodes. It does not necessarily exist (this is to be defined during simulation) or can be merged with any other node.

**Context:** Information that can be used to describe the current environmental conditions of a certain object, we use definition proposed by Dey at el. (2001) and in two papers of Brezillon (1999).

**Design Phase:** At the design phase nodes become aware of other nodes' accessible information storages and acceptable predicates.

**Domain Ontology:** A detailed specification of the model of the main domain of interest; it includes the vocabulary (i.e. a list of logical constants and predicate symbols) to describe the domain and a set of logical expressions, definition of the constraints existing in the given domain and rules for interpretation of the vocabulary.

**Fog Computing:** An architecture that uses collaborative multitude of the user clients and devices located in the user's proximity to carry out major part of processing, storage and communication tasks related to delivery of services to the user.

**Information Fragment:** An information unit extended by the "precondition" statement, which defines when the appropriate information unit is valid, and also might include the "post-condition" statement. The post-condition is aimed to describe what is supposed to be done when the precondition is met the information unit is hold. Each information fragment may consist of several preconditions, information units and post-conditions.

**Information Storage:** A logical unit for collecting information units.

**Information Unit (Subject, Predicate, Object):** IU represents a logical expression: "subject"-"predicate"-"object" = [true | false]. Subject is usually an actor (human or node that performs or is supposed to perform a certain action, e.g. a multimedia centre). Predicate is an action that has to be performed (e.g., "playing music"). Object points to the target with which the action has to be performed (e.g., a song being played).

**Interface (I/F):** Provides information exchange between nodes and information storages. The interface is considered as fully reliable without any delay or energy costs. In this reference model the interface performs a technical function of connecting nodes to information storages. It does not implement logical functions and does not affect information transfer costs.

**Internet of Things (IoT):** The internetworking of IoT devices that enable these devices to collect and exchange data for achieving a common goal.

**IoT Device:** A physical device embedded with electronics, software, sensors, actuators, and network connectivity sufficient for collecting and exchanging data with other devices.

**Knowledge Corpus:** Defines the smart spaces structure that consist of a set of shared resources including data and data processing function, which continuously performs data mining operations for extracting new relevant knowledge and performing routine monitoring functions based on the target functions set by the user or smart space services.

**Node Profile:** Stores information about nodes.

**Node:** A logical unit capable to perform some actions depending on information units stored in accessible information storages. In many practical implementations of smart spaces nodes are represented by agents.

**Runtime Phase:** At the runtime phase the nodes exchange information units in accordance with the scenario and behavior rules.

**Service Intelligence:** A measurement of an ability of a service to adopt behavior to the environment without human intervention.

**Smart Environment:** A concept of the physical world that is richly and invisibly interwoven with sensors, actuators, displays, and computational elements, embedded seamlessly in the everyday objects of our lives, and connected through a continuous network.

**Smart Space:** A set of communicating nodes and information storages, which has embedded logic to acquire and apply knowledge about its environment and adapt to its inhabitants in order to improve their experience in the environment.

**Smart-M3:** An open-source software platform that aims to provide a smart spaces infrastructure. It combines the ideas of distributed, networked systems and semantic web. The ultimate goal is to enable smart environments and linking of real and virtual worlds.

**User Node:** Responsible for interaction with a user. It can be considered as user's personal assistant.

**User Profiles:** Contain information about the users.

Chapter 2

# The M3 Architecture
# for Smart Spaces

## ABSTRACT

*In accordance with the previous chapter, a particular class of smart environments is created by Smart Spaces, where many devices participate using information-driven and ontology-oriented interaction. In this case, a smart space is developed based on models from multi-agent systems and knowledge manipulation technologies from the Semantic Web. In this chapter, we consider this particular approach for creating such smart environments. The M3 architecture (multidevice, multivendor, multidomain) aims at development of smart spaces that host advanced service-oriented applications. We introduce the theoretical background of the M3 architecture in respect to its open source implementation—the Smart-M3 platform. The latter forms a technology for creating M3-based smart spaces (M3 spaces) as heterogeneous dynamic multi-agent systems with multi-device, multi-vendor, multi-domain devices and services. We further consider the concept models of space computing that enable the studied class of smart spaces, derive the generic properties that an M3 space design requires, and describe the basic software components of M3 architecture that realize the generic design properties in accordance with the concept models.*

DOI: 10.4018/978-1-5225-2653-7.ch002

# INTRODUCTION

As we showed in the previous chapter, the smart spaces paradigm aims at application development for advanced computing environments, when participating objects acquire and apply knowledge for service construction in order to enhance user experience, quality and reliability of the provided information (Balandin & Waris, 2009; Augusto, Callaghan, Cook, Kameas, & Satoh, 2013). Each participating object is represented with a software agent—an autonomous information processing unit, which is not necessarily attached to a fixed device. Software are of adjustable autonomy agents (Ball & Callaghan, 2012). They run on various devices of the environment and represent smart space participants acting as knowledge processors for semantic-driven information sharing (Kiljander, Ylisaukko-oja, Takalo-Mattila, Etelapera, & Soininen, 2012). A service is constructed by joint activity of interacting agents (Balandin et al., 2010). The interaction is indirect, in contrast to the communication level provided by the IoT technology (i.e., no need in direct agent-to-agent communication). Agents joint activity creates a service construction chain. At the end of the chain a meaningful information value is shaped to deliver it as a service to the users (Korzun, 2014).

In this chapter, we consider the M3 architecture to applying smart space paradigm for interaction of different devices and information & computation resources on the interoperability level (Korzun, Kashevnik, Balandin, & Smirnov, 2015). The abbreviation "M3" stands for Multidevice, Multivendor, and Multidomain. The M3 architecture is based on the disruptive technologies coming from two innovative concepts: the Semantic Web (SW) and the Internet of Things (IoT). SW concept was born to drive the Web towards the original Tim Berners Lee's vision, the so-called web of data (Berners-Lee, Hendler, & Lassila, 2001). The SW technology stack is primarily composed by technologies allowing the representation (RDF, RDFS, OWL) and retrieval (SPARQL) of semantically annotated data (Gutierrez, Hurtado, Mendelzon, & Perez, 2011). The IoT concept is a large-scale evolution of the innovative vision of Mark Weiser about ubiquitous computing (Weiser, 1991): the Internet, in addition to personal desktops and mobile computers, is also populated with billions of heterogeneous interconnected smart devices, which represent (and advance) physical things. Everyday life objects, alongside traditional computers, become smart objects—data processors and service constructors to their users (Kortuem, Kawsar, Sundramoorthy, & Fitton, 2010; Gubbi, Buyya, Marusic, & Palaniswami, 2013).

The Smart-M3 platform is an open source solution that implements the M3 architecture for smart space development and deployment in various computing environments (Honkola, Laine, Brown, & Tyrkko, 2010). Service construction in such an M3 space is based on agent-based participation with information sharing for cooperative knowledge processing by participants themselves, either human or machines (Korzun, 2016). This approach supports localization and interconnection of available resources, their semantics, and information-driven programming over this dynamic knowledge corpus. Therefore, an M3 space provides an information hub to support indirect information-driven interactions of the participating agents. Information-driven perception and recognition becomes the primary mechanism in an application: the notion of a service emerges from activities and capabilities of the agents, including those agents that represent end-user activity.

This M3 variant of smart spaces is based on the success stories of several projects funded by European commission (European Neighborhood and Partnership Instrument, cross border cooperation, and DIGILE IoT SHOK program). In these activities, the M3 architecture for smart spaces was developed with the priority on promoting the openness and with the focus on the interoperability. The Smart-M3 platform has been initially developed by a consortium of companies within research projects Artemis JU funded SOFIA project (Smart Objects for Intelligent Applications) and Finnish nationally funded program DIEM (Device Interoperability Ecosystem). Smart-M3 was released as open source platform at the NoTA Conference on October 1, 2009. Soon after its first release, the Smart-M3 potential was understood and applied in other European research and development projects (e.g., in eHealth, eMobility, smart cities). Furthermore, EIT ICT Labs, an Innovation Factory for ICT Innovation in Europe, included smart spaces among its innovation areas. At the moment, the main developers of Smart-M3 platform are several communities, including Open Innovations Association FRUCT (http://fruct.org/) with its consortium of European and Russian universities, academy, and industry partners.

# BACKGROUND: ENABLER CONCEPT MODELS

A typical smart space-based application can be considered as a cyber-physical system (Ning, Liu, Ma, Yang, & Huang, 2016). It is an engineered system based on seamless integration of computational resources (information world) and physical components (physical world). Example applications are remote collaboration (Takada, Sakurai, Knauf, & Tsuruta, 2012), parking support (Smirnov, Shilov, & Gusikhin, 2016), infomobility in tourism domain (Smirnov, Shilov, Kashevnik, & Ponomarev, 2017), and cybermedicine (Korzun, 2017). The layered structure of service-oriented system design is shown in Figure 1, where the central role is designated to information processing and related semantics (Korzun, 2016).

The basic idea is using the IoT technology to transform entities of the physical world into smart objects: such a physical entity is augmented with computing and networking capabilities (Kortuem, Kawsar, Sundramoorthy, & Fitton, 2010). The term "smart" for an object designates the basic intelligence attributes: each object acts autonomously making own decisions, senses the environment, communicates with other objects, accesses resources of the existing Internet and Web, and interacts with users. As a result, a new type of ubiquitous computing environments appears, where each environment is formed by many heterogeneous digital objects. An important class of objects is made by personal mobile devices such as tablets, smartphones, and various gadgets (Korzun, Balandin, 2016). This way, resources from the physical, cyber and social worlds are fused into a network communication system.

*Figure 1. Layers of a service-oriented cyber-physical system*

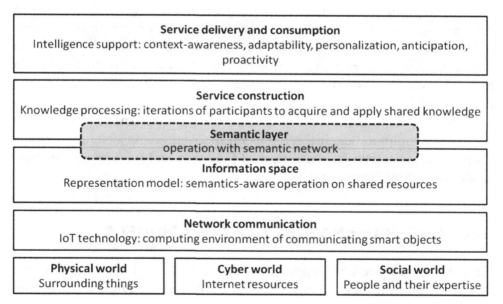

Based on the general case of a smart or intelligent environment, a smart space focuses rather on service and information aspects (Korzun, 2016), rather than on underlying digital equipment as it happens in IoT. A smart space supports the ability to acquire and apply knowledge about the environment as a whole and all its users in order to improve their experience of service consumption in that environment (Balandin & Waris, 2009). First, a common information space is created. Second, service construction applies knowledge processing in this information space. Consequently, the term "smart" for a digital environment designates that activity of participating objects makes the environment intelligence in the form of advanced services. Within such an environment, its smart objects create a smart space by constructing and delivering value added digital services. Each object (being a smart one) reasons about, controls, and adapts to physical surroundings and user context. Individual operation of an object follows a typical cycle of (i) perceiving the state of the environment, (ii) reasoning about the state together with application goals and outcomes of possible actions, and (iii) acting upon the environment to change the state. Intelligence support is implemented within service delivery and consumption, focusing on such properties as context-awareness, adaptability, personalization, anticipation, proactivity.

In the simplest case, a smart object constructs a service based solely on own direct observations (e.g., by sensors the device has). That is, such an object acts as a provider of one or more services. (They are also called smart services). An advanced case appears when service construction is based on cooperative activity: several objects collect and share common knowledge about available resources of the environment and about semantics of ongoing processes. In particular, space-based computing declares this style of interactions (Nixon, Simperl, Krummenacher, & Martin-Recuerda, 2008), which is closely related to multi-agent systems (Gorodetsky, 2013) and autonomic computing (Bicevskis, Bicevska, Rauhvargers, Oditis, & Borzovs, 2015). Each agent can publish and retrieve data into/from a shared information space. An application is organized as an ad-hoc composition of software agents interacting indirectly by information sharing.

The basic space-based communication model is extended by concretizing a way of information representation. Triple space computing applies the Semantic Web technologies, which aim at making information on the Web readable by both humans and machines (Horrocks, 2008). RDF triples are basic information representation units in the form of subject-predicate-object

(Gutierrez, Hurtado, Mendelzon, & Perez, 2011). They in turn are organized into RDF graphs with subjects and objects as nodes and predicates as links, i.e., forming semantic-rich information structures kept in RDF triplestores. Ontologies become primary tools for manipulating with such structures. Advanced queries become possible, utilizing RDF reasoning capabilities and semantic query languages like SPARQL. As a result, a space-localized knowledge base is created targeted to the needs of web applications. The Semantic Web technologies provide a clear way to achieve the information interoperability and to enable integration, communication, and coordination of many heterogeneous service providers and consumers.

The model of conceptual spaces—Cspaces (Martín-Recuerda, 2005)—improves triple space computing to be applicable in different scenarios apart from web services. CSpaces extend the publish-based model with pub/sub model and transaction support to guarantee successful execution of a group of operations. The subscription operation provides effective means for an agent to detect changes in the shared information space and then to react accordingly. The CSpaces model makes control flow decoupling from the agent side, which is done in addition to time and space decoupling of the publish-based model. In this model, service construction is an iterative process for agents to collectively produce information. Such information provides a user with knowledge to apply (e.g., recommendation on nearby attractions for a tourist) or an object with commands to execute (e.g., changing lighting in the room). Notably that the knowledge-aware pub/sub model suits well for the needs of Big Data analytics across multiple heterogeneous systems scattered throughout the Internet (Esposito, Ficco, Palmieri, & Castiglione, 2015; Roffia et al., 2016).

Information collected in the same space can be further processed, providing knowledge that otherwise cannot be available from a single source. Any agent can infer new facts as a reaction to information that has been published by others. This iterative information-driven model supports cooperative knowledge acquisition for service construction and applying this knowledge in service delivery and consumption. Appropriate decision-making components are based on AmI (Ambient intelligence) methods and technology (Spanoudakis & Moraitis, 2015; Yachir, Amirat, Chibani, & Badache, 2016). This approach leads to opportunity to create increasingly complex and flexibly deployed applications, where the term "smart" designates such intelligence properties as context-aware service construction, service adaptability and personalization, anticipation on needed services and their proactive delivery.

# GENERIC DESIGN PROPERTIES

Recall that a smart space is defined as a virtual, service-centric, multi-user, multi-device, dynamic-interaction information system that applies a shared view of resources to create a smart (intelligent) environment (Augusto, Callaghan, Cook, Kameas, & Satoh, 2013). Such a system implements the information level of smart environment on top of its devices, resources, and networks. The underlying computing environment is typically localized being associated with a physical spatial-restricted place (e.g., room, home, city square). In contrast to more generic notion of a smart environment, the term "space" is treated rather an information space than a physical space, i.e., a smart space implements an associative memory for participants.

The smart spaces approach supports the following generic design properties for applications in smart environments (Korzun, 2016): a) agent-based participation of the involved objects, b) information hub for multi-party semantics-aware operation, c) information-driven perception and recognition for service construction and delivery.

- **Agent-Based Participation:** Each smart space participant is represented by a software agent—a programmed autonomous computational process, which is responsible for a distinguishable portion of the application logic and executing on some device. A smart space participant is not strictly associated with a particular host device and less focused on the underlying network communication means. Similarly, to the notion of "agent" from multi-agent systems, a smart space participant can 1) identify itself as a part of the environment and application, 2) understand environment and application state, 3) operate with a certain part of the shared knowledge, and 4) make over this part own interpretations, decisions, and actions. In contrast, such agents are of adjustable autonomy, allowing the trade-off between the level of convenience offered by autonomous behavior and the amount of control offered by application needs and user driven activity.
- **Information Hub:** A smart space provides as an information hub to support indirect information-driven interactions of the participants. The latter (by means of their agents) are able to exchange information in the smart space, to reason knowledge and make decisions using this information and in accordance with the application needs and with user driven activity. Each agent produces its share of information and

makes it available to others via the hub. Similarly, the agent consumes information of its own interest from the hub. As a result, there is no need to establish many paired agent-to-agent connections. No knowledge is required on how the published information fragment is then used and by whom. The distinguishable property is that such an information hub implements an environment knowledge base. Instead of duplication of resources from multiple sources, the semantics of resources are kept. This way, the smart space keeps virtualized and digitalized representation of the concerned parts of the physical and information worlds. Advanced mechanisms, such as search and persistent queries, are provided for agents to effectively process the shared representation. In particularly, any smart space participant has access to the information physically distributed over many digital devices and data sources.

- **Information-Driven Perception and Recognition:** In a smart spaces-based application the notion of a service emerges from activities and capabilities of the agents, including those agents that represent end-user activity. A scenario defines a control flow initiated from the user side (explicit or implicit detection of user needs) and completed at a point where the user perceives a service to consume (something for satisfaction of the needs). The consumption can be in the form of information visualized to the user (e.g., a recommendation is provided) or the user observes some changes in the environment (e.g., room lighting becomes lower). A scenario control flow is information-driven, generalizing the event-driven programming model. It assumes "do something if certain knowledge is recognized". The reasoning mechanisms are based on deductive closure and allow continuously defining new semantic relations between information fragments in the information hub. Each agent is able to extract hidden knowledge, which can be further integrated into the interconnected knowledge corpus. Agents perceive the application-aware activity by recognition of changes (new events and derived facts) and then react to contribute to service construction and delivery.

Let us further in this chapter consider how these generic design properties are realized using the M3 architecture, in respect to its open source implementation—the Smart-M3 platform (Honkola, Laine, Brown, & Tyrkko, 2010; Viola, D'Elia, Korzun, Galov, Kashevnik, & Balandin, 2016).

# THE M3 ARCHITECTURE

The M3 architecture for smart spaces focuses on the interoperability properties, supporting devices and other resources fused in the smart space to open their information for others in a machine interpretable format (Kiljander, Ylisaukko-oja, Takalo-Mattila, Etelapera, & Soininen, 2012; Ovaska, Cinotti, & Toninelli, 2012). The architecture defines an interoperable information sharing platform (middleware) for deploying smart spaces. The platform specifies a device, application, and service domain independent way to access the smart spaces, exploiting the ontology-oriented models and technologies of the Semantic Web for information representation. The M3 architecture intentionally emphasizes the term "knowledge" since 1) a smart space operates with multi-domain and meta information (habitual data, relations between them, computations), 2) these heterogeneous data are semantically linked, and thus 3) the agents interact over the interconnected knowledge corpus. The latter is also called a semantic network since it forms the basic mathematical model for data mining in smart space, e.g., see (Korzun, Marchenkov, Vdovenko, & Petrina, 2016).

The M3 architecture defines the three basic components as Figure 2 shows: Semantic Information Broker (SIB), Smart Space Access Protocol (SSAP),

*Figure 2. Basic M3 space components*

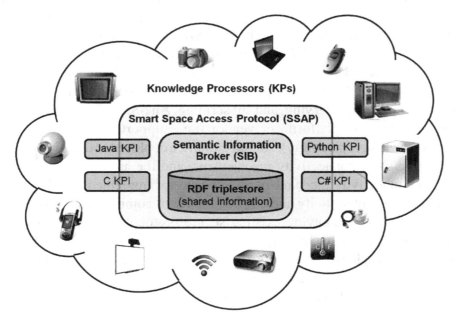

and Knowledge Processor (KP). A particular software implementation of the M3 architecture is Smart-M3 (Honkola, Laine, Brown, & Tyrkko, 2010), which is open source. We shall use the term "M3 space" when the smart space is built using the Smart-M3 platform. Any M3 space forms a named information search extension for interacting participants.

A standalone SIB implements an information hub forming a logical rendezvous and information-level interoperability infrastructure on the top of an RDF triplestore (or a SPARQL endpoint). SIB acts as an access point to the information hub of the M3 space (Viola, D'Elia, Korzun, Galov, Kashevnik, & Balandin, 2016). In particular, SIB becomes responsible for network connections from M3 space participants, management of incoming queries, and operation transit with the underlying RDF triplestore. To implement a capable smart space the SIB needs a powerful host computer. Nevertheless, the M3 architecture does not prevent construction of tiny smart spaces (e.g., SIB runs on a local Wi-Fi router or on a personal smartphone). An M3 space, created by its SIB, has own symbolic name and is addressable by IP address and port of the SIB. Additional components can implement M3 space discovery for participants. Publicly or privately accessed SIBs can be used to create custom smart spaces in accordance with the application needs. Also, SIB is responsible for governance of the shared information, including concurrent and authorized access control. For instance, access to a given fragment is restricted or the owner is specified. Additional security and privacy mechanisms are possible, e.g., those that proposed in RIBS (RDF Information Base Solution)—another M3 SIB software implementation.

Communication with SIB follows the SSAP rules and syntax, recently generalized to Knowledge Sharing Protocol (KSP), see (Kiljander, Morandi, & Soininen, 2012). The protocol provides read&write operations for inserting, removing, updating, querying, and subscribing. An SSAP client is not bound to any device type, platform, or vendor (i.e., supporting the device- and network-level interoperability). Architecturally, a deployed SIB can have many different network connectivity mechanisms, and the application developer selects a connectivity mechanism appropriate for implementing KP on the target devices. Authenticity and confidentiality of communication with SIB can be achieved by applying existing secure protocols, e.g., Host Identity Protocol (HIP) or Transport Layer Security (TLS) protocol.

Each KP implements a software agent that represents an M3 space participant. The focus is rather on cooperative knowledge processing over shared information than on autonomous participation in the smart space.

This way, a KP acts as an agent of adjustable autonomy (Ball & Callaghan, 2012). Knowledge Processor Interface (KPI) implements the functionality that enables KP to interact in the M3 space: SSAP client part, primitives for local manipulation with shared information, functions for security and reliability, etc. KPI libraries are Smart-M3 middleware for application development of KP code. They are available for many programming languages (e.g., Python, C, Java, C#). The M3 architecture defines an application as an ad-hoc assembly of KPs. A schematic view on a smart space hosting several cross-domain applications is shown in Figure 3.

One or more M3 spaces can be used to implement collaboratively a service scenario to meet users' goal. The generic view is illustrated in Figure 4. Each space is maintained by own set of SIBs to host a certain suite of applications. Each application consists of several KPs that publish and query the shared information depending on observing actions of each other. Some KPs are wrappers for external systems; some are used for knowledge exchange between the M3 spaces. Scenario steps emerge from actions taken by the KPs and observable in their M3 space. The information-driven perception and recognition allow composable scenarios from multiple applications, i.e., the knowledge deduced in one scenario can be reused in other scenarios. The coupling between the participating KPs is loose limiting the impact of each

*Figure 3. A smart space hosting several applications as ad-hoc assemblies of KPs*

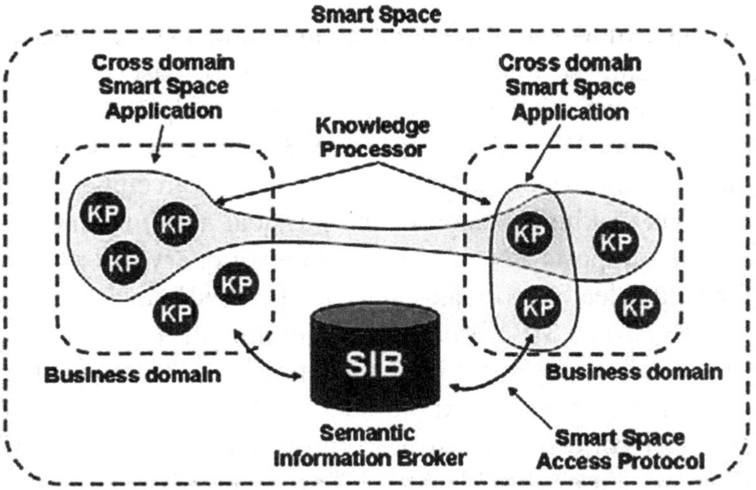

*Figure 4. A system of M3 spaces hosting own service-oriented applications*

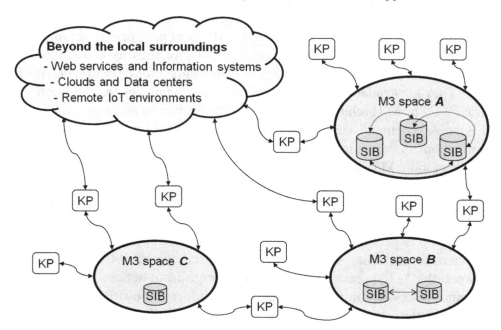

KP to others by the knowledge the KP shares. For reasoning and deduction the KP may consolidate locally its private (non-published in the space) and shared (from the space) information. The derived knowledge can be selectively published in the M3 space.

The semantic interoperability for many information producers and consumers are achieved due to the RDF model for describing the shared information, i.e., adopting the low-level (machine interpretable) triple-based approach of Semantic Web. Consequently, M3 space provides operation with an interconnected knowledge corpus, which spans from embedded domains to the Web, thus making a fusion of the physical and information worlds. In addition, SIB supports advanced operations for query and processing the shared information, leading to a full-valued RDF-based knowledge base. If SIB supports SPARQL then SIB acts a SPARQL endpoint. Any KP can query the knowledge base and make non-trivial reasoning over the knowledge corpus. The latest Smart-M3 releases exploit such RDF triplestore frameworks as Redland (http://librdf.org) and Virtuoso (http://virtuoso.openlinksw.com).

The M3 architecture is based on the following properties of interoperable and seamless participation within a smart spaces-based application.

- Shared view of available resources and services using RDF representation.
- Integration of various devices and other objects of the physical and information worlds.
- Semantic-driven access to and operation with information coming from multiple sources.
- Reasoning and decision-making over collectively operated knowledge corpus.

To achieve these properties the following M3 space design principles are established to guide application development.

- Define localization of the environment.
- Create virtualization of participating objects and ongoing processes.
- Operate with semantic information on available resources.
- Let participation be information-driven.

The principle of localization influences the application architecture and layout when KPs are selected and assigned to local devices. The principle of virtualization enables creating a shared informational model of the recent system state accessible and understandable by application KPs. The principle of semantics-aware operation moves the design beyond traditional service-oriented information systems with regular databases. The principle of information-driven participation reduces a KP design to specifying: what information to perceive, what knowledge to recognize, what action to react.

These design principles are a result of systematization of our previous application development experience, see (Korzun, Kashevnik, Balandin, & Smirnov, 2015). We consider them as a base for a certain methodology for smart spaces-based application development. Importantly that the principles lead to the following key features for applications: (1) interoperability support for a multitude of participated heterogeneous devices, services, and users localized in the physical surroundings and (2) personalized and proactive behavior and coordination in digital service construction and delivery. Further in Chapter 3 we consider how the principles work in the emerging case of IoT environments. To form a methodology of smart spaces-based application development the principles are augmented with ontology-oriented modeling techniques as we show further in Chapter 4. Use cases from our application development experience are considered in Chapter 5 to illustrate the applicability of the proposed design principles. In particular, we show the principle of localization using the SmartRoom system design, when many mobile end-users collaboratively work in a multimedia-equipped room. The principle of virtualization is applied in the SmartScribo system design, when the blogosphere is partially virtualized in the M3 space. The principle of information-driven participation is used in the Ridesharing application design, when interests of several persons are matched with the appropriate driver.

## SOLUTIONS AND RECOMMENDATIONS

Table 1 summarizes the design principles that the M3 architecture provides to guide applications development. Each principle is complemented with particular properties showing possible ways of the use in smart spaces-based application development using the Smart-M3 platform.

## FUTURE RESEARCH DIRECTIONS

The M3 architecture provides certain design principles to guide applications development. Although we shall consider examples of their application in the subsequent chapters, the area of methods for development and programming M3 spaces needs more elaboration, systematization, unification, and formalization. Each principle should be covered by a set of matured methods in respect to efficient practical use.

## CONCLUSION

This chapter overviewed the M3 architecture and its open source implementation in the Smart-M3 platform. The M3 architecture is based on enabler models for smart spaces. The models support the generic design properties for application development in smart environments. The M3 architecture further focuses on the interoperability properties, supporting devices and other resources, fused in the smart space, to open their information for others. To achieve these properties the M3 space design principles are established to guide smart space-based application development. The principles lead to the following key features for applications: (1) interoperability support for a

*Table 1. Design principles of application development for M3 spaces*

| Principle | Description | Properties |
|---|---|---|
| Define localization of the environment | The growing number of devices makes the role of local resources essential for a smart space created in the environment. Although any resource in the Internet is potentially accessible from the environment, the major part of data producers can concentrate locally, on the Internet edge. | • Surrounding devices are primary participants.<br>• An essential corpus of situational and personalized information is generated locally.<br>• Access to the Internet enhances the system.<br>• Personal devices (carried, wearable, etc.) are of uttermost importance.<br>• Mobile devices concern the major share of participants. |
| Create virtualization of participating objects and ongoing processes | Since a smart space is a system consisting of many participants (local or remote, from physical or information worlds), the system structure can be represented in the smart space as shared information. Such representation also covers situational, behavioral, and evolutional attributes of participants and their joint activity. This type of virtualization leads to a dynamic network formed in the smart space to reflect the overall system state. The network is semantic following the ontology of application domain in the physical and information worlds. | • Any participant has its digital representation in the smart space.<br>• Problem domain objects and processes are also represented.<br>• Data sources are represented virtually (no raw data duplication).<br>• Relations between participants, domain objects, and processes are represented, including context. |
| Operate with semantic information on available resources | Shared information is a knowledge corpus where a multitude of heterogeneous information fragments are interconnected (dynamically and sparsely). This case is different from a regular database: information represents rather hidden knowledge that need to be derived than an explicitly stored fragment that can be literally extracted. | • Establishing relations between information fragments create the semantics.<br>• Description of the way to access information is shared, instead of the original information fragments.<br>• Search operations based on semantic-specified query are the primary reasoning mechanism. |
| Let participation be information-driven | One form of participation is perception when the participant detects a specified part of shared information (i.e., the case of a smart object that understands its recent state in the environment). More advanced form is recognition when the participant extracts (hidden) knowledge from the shared (and local) information (e.g., to recognize a situation where it can help or when it is allowed to offer help). | • Participation is information-driven, by perception and recognition of knowledge formed in the M3 space.<br>• Services are composable: the shared information is usable by many services constructed in the M3 space.<br>• Service delivery is proactive when the need in the service is recognized in the M3 space. |

multitude of participated heterogeneous devices, services, and users localized in the physical surroundings and (2) personalized and proactive behavior and coordination in service construction and delivery.

# REFERENCES

Augusto, J. C., Callaghan, V., Cook, D., Kameas, A., & Satoh, I. (2013). Intelligent Environments: A manifesto. *Human-centric Computing and Information Sciences*, *3*(12), 1–18.

Balandin, S., Oliver, I., Boldyrev, S., Smirnov, A., Kashevnik, A., & Shilov, N. (2010). Anonymous Agent Coordination in Smart Spaces. *Proceedings of The Fourth International Conference on Mobile Ubiquitous Computing, Systems, Services and Technologies* (pp. 242-246). IARIA.

Balandin, S., & Waris, H. (2009). Key Properties in the Development of Smart Spaces. *Proceedings of International Conference on Universal Access in Human-Computer Interaction. Intelligent and Ubiquitous Interaction Environments, LNCS* (Vol. 5615, pp. 3-12). Springer. doi:10.1007/978-3-642-02710-9_1

Ball, M., & Callaghan, V. (2012). Managing Control, Convenience and Autonomy - A Study of Agent Autonomy in Intelligent Environments. In T. Bosse (Ed), Agents and Ambient Intelligence (Vol. 12, pp. 159-196). IOS Press.

Berners-Lee, T., Hendler, J., & Lassila, O. (2001). The semantic web. *Scientific American, 284*(5), 28–37. doi:10.1038/scientificamerican0501-34 PMID:11341160

Bicevskis, J., Bicevska, Z., Rauhvargers, K., Oditis, I., & Borzovs, J. (2015). A Practitioner's Approach to Achieve Autonomic Computing Goals. *Baltic Journal of Modern Computing, 3*(4), 273–293.

Esposito, C., Ficco, M., Palmieri, F., & Castiglione, A. (2015). A knowledge-based platform for Big Data analytics based on publish-subscribe services and stream processing. *Knowledge-Based Systems, 79*(C), 3–17. doi:10.1016/j.knosys.2014.05.003

Gorodetsky, V. (2013). Agents and Distributed Data Mining in Smart Space. *Proceedings of International Workshop on Agents and Data Mining Interaction, LNCS* (Vol. 7607, pp. 153-165). Springer. doi:10.1007/978-3-642-36288-0_14

Gubbi, J., Buyya, R., Marusic, S., & Palaniswami, M. (2013). Internet of Things (IoT): A vision, architectural elements, and future directions. *Future Generation Computer Systems, 29*(7), 1645–1660. doi:10.1016/j.future.2013.01.010

Gutierrez, C., Hurtado, C. A., Mendelzon, A. O., & Perez, J. (2011). Foundations of Semantic Web databases. *Journal of Computer and System Sciences, 77*(3), 520–541. doi:10.1016/j.jcss.2010.04.009

Honkola, J., Laine, H., Brown, R., & Tyrkko, O. (2010). Smart-M3 Information Sharing Platform. *Proceedings of The IEEE symposium on Computers and Communications* (pp. 1041-1046). IEEE. doi:10.1109/ISCC.2010.5546642

Horrocks, I. (2008). Ontologies and the Semantic Web. *Communications of the ACM, 51*(12), 58–67. doi:10.1145/1409360.1409377

Kiljander, J., Morandi, F., & Soininen, J.-P. (2012). Knowledge Sharing Protocol for Smart Spaces. *International Journal of Advanced Computer Science and Applications, 3*(9), 100–110. doi:10.14569/IJACSA.2012.030915

Kiljander, J., Ylisaukko-oja, A., Takalo-Mattila, J., Etelapera, M., & Soininen, J.-P. (2012). Enabling Semantic Technology Empowered Smart Spaces. *Journal of Computer Networks and Communications, 2012*, 1–14. doi:10.1155/2012/845762

Kortuem, G., Kawsar, F., Sundramoorthy, V., & Fitton, D. (2010). Smart objects as building blocks for the Internet of Things. *IEEE Internet Computing, 14*(1), 44–51. doi:10.1109/MIC.2009.143

Korzun, D. (2014). Service Formalism and Architectural Abstractions for Smart Space Applications. *Proceedings of the 10th Central and Eastern European Software Engineering Conference in Russia* (pp. 1-7). ACM. doi:10.1145/2687233.2687253

Korzun, D. (2016). On the Smart Spaces Approach to Semantic-driven Design of Service-oriented Information Systems. *Proceedings of the International Baltic Conference on Databases and Information Systems, CCIS* (Vol. 615, pp. 181-195). Springer International Publishing. doi:10.1007/978-3-319-40180-5_13

Korzun, D. (2017). Internet of things meets mobile health systems in smart spaces: An overview. In C. Bhatt, N. Dey, & A. S. Ashour (Eds.), Internet of Things and Big Data Technologies for Next Generation Healthcare (Vol. 23, pp. 111-129). Springer International Publishing.

Korzun, D., & Balandin, S. (2016). Personalizing the Internet of Things Using Mobile Information Services. *Proceedings of The Tenth International Conference on Mobile Ubiquitous Computing, Systems, Services and Technologies* (pp. 184-189). IARIA.

Korzun, D., Kashevnik, A., Balandin, S., & Smirnov, A. (2015). The Smart-M3 Platform: Experience of Smart Space Application Development for Internet of Things. *Proceedings of Internet of Things, Smart Spaces, and Next Generation Networks and Systems: 15th International Conference NEW2AN 2015 and 8th Conference ruSMART 2015, LNCS* (Vol. 9247, pp. 56-67). Springer International Publishing.

Korzun, D. G., Marchenkov, S. A., Vdovenko, A. S., & Petrina, O. B. (2016). A Semantic Approach to Designing Information Services for Smart Museums. *International Journal of Embedded and Real-Time Communication Systems*, 7(2), 15–34. doi:10.4018/IJERTCS.2016070102

Martín-Recuerda, F. (2005). Towards Cspaces: A new perspective for the Semantic Web. *Proceedings of 1st IFIP WG12.5 Working Conference of Industrial Applications of Semantic Web* (Vol. 188, pp. 113-139). Springer. doi:10.1007/0-387-29248-9_7

Ning, H., Liu, H., Ma, J., Yang, L. T., & Huang, R. (2016). Cybermatics: Cyber-physical-social-thinking hyperspace based science and technology. *Future Generation Computer Systems*, 56(C), 504–522. doi:10.1016/j.future.2015.07.012

Nixon, L. J. B., Simperl, E., Krummenacher, R., & Martin-Recuerda, F. (2008). Tuplespace-based Computing for the Semantic Web: A Survey of the State-of-the-Art. *The Knowledge Engineering Review*, 23(2), 181–212. doi:10.1017/S0269888907001221

Ovaska, E., Cinotti, T. S., & Toninelli, A. (2012). The Design Principles and Practices of Interoperable Smart Spaces. In X. Liu & Y. Li (Eds.), Advanced Design Approaches to Emerging Software Systems: Principles, Methodologies and Tools (pp. 18–47). Hershey, PA: IGI Global. doi:10.4018/978-1-60960-735-7.ch002

Roffia, L., Morandi, F., Kiljander, J., DElia, A., Vergari, F., Viola, F., & Cinotti, T. S. et al. (2016). A Semantic Publish-Subscribe Architecture for the Internet of Things. *IEEE Internet of Things Journal*, 3(6), 1274–1296. doi:10.1109/JIOT.2016.2587380

Smirnov, A., Shilov, N., & Gusikhin, O. (2016). Socio-Cyberphysical System for Parking Support. *International Journal of Future Computer and Communication*, 5(1), 27–32. doi:10.18178/ijfcc.2016.5.1.438

Smirnov, A., Shilov, N., Kashevnik, A., & Ponomarev, A. (2017). Cyber-physical infomobility for tourism application. *International Journal of Information Technology and Management*, *16*(1), 31–52. doi:10.1504/IJITM.2017.080949

Spanoudakis, N., & Moraitis, P. (2015). Engineering ambient intelligence systems using agent technology. *IEEE Intelligent Systems*, *30*(3), 60–67. doi:10.1109/MIS.2015.3

Takada, K., Sakurai, Y., Knauf, R., & Tsuruta, S. (2012). Enriched Cyberspace Through Adaptive Multimedia Utilization for Dependable Remote Collaboration. *IEEE Transactions on Systems, Man, and Cybernetics. Part A, Systems and Humans*, *42*(5), 1026–1039. doi:10.1109/TSMCA.2012.2183588

Viola, F., D'Elia, A., Korzun, D., Galov, I., Kashevnik, A., & Balandin, S. (2016). The M3 Architecture for Smart Spaces: Overview of Semantic Information Broker Implementations. *Proceedings of 19th Conference of Open Innovations Association FRUCT* (pp. 264-272). IEEE. doi:10.23919/FRUCT.2016.7892210

Weiser, M. (1991). The computer for the 21st century. *Scientific American*, *265*(3), 94–104. doi:10.1038/scientificamerican0991-94 PMID:1675486

Yachir, A., Amirat, Y., Chibani, A., & Badache, N. (2016). Event-Aware Framework for Dynamic Services Discovery and Selection in the Context of Ambient Intelligence and Internet of Things. *IEEE Transactions on Automation Science and Engineering*, *13*(1), 85–102. doi:10.1109/TASE.2015.2499792

## KEY TERMS AND DEFINITIONS

**Information Hub:** The connection or integration point for information derived from multiple data sources.

**Information-Driven Participation:** The rule "do something if a certain event occurs" (event-driven) or "do something if certain knowledge becomes available" in the advanced case.

**Knowledge Processor (KP):** A self-programming pre-emptive process that is executed autonomously on some device for the needs of information processing and knowledge derivation. One of the central component of the M3 architecture.

**Semantic Information Broker (SIB):** A server that implements information hub for multiple knowledge processors. One of the central component of the M3 architecture.

**Service Construction:** A process of cooperative activity of knowledge processors over the shared information. In the result, an information fragment is created, which can be delivered to the users for further visualization, interpretation, and decision-making.

**Service Delivery:** Provision of an information fragment to the users and using appropriate device. The information fragment is further visualized and interpreted by the users themselves.

**Smart Space:** A virtual, service-centric, multi-user, multi-device, dynamic-interaction information system that applies a shared view of resources to create a smart (intelligent) environment.

# Chapter 3
# M3 Spaces in Internet of Things Environments

## ABSTRACT

*As we showed in the previous chapter, the M3 architecture supports the Smart Spaces concept with localization and interconnection of available resources, their semantics, and information-driven programming over this dynamic knowledge corpus (in the form of a semantic network). In this chapter, we consider the settings of IoT environments. The settings play an essential practical role, influencing the way how an M3 space and its applications are deployed on the existing networked equipment of a given IoT environment. Basically, IoT refers to the connection of physical objects. IoT technologies make all the devices of a spatial-limited physical computing environment interconnected as well as connected to the Internet. This ability leads to the consideration of notion of localized IoT-environments which now appears in many places of everyday life. Software agents running on devices turn the latter into "smart objects" that are visible in our daily lives as real participating entities. As a result, the next generation of software applications (smart applications) can be deployed in localized IoT-environments in the form of M3 spaces.*

DOI: 10.4018/978-1-5225-2653-7.ch003

# INTRODUCTION

In contrast to Giant Global Graph of the Semantic Web, M3 spaces are of local and dynamic nature (Oliver, 2008). This property suits well for the Internet of Things (IoT) with its ubiquitous interconnections of highly heterogeneous networked entities and networks (Kortuem, Kawsar, Sundramoorthy, & Fitton, 2010). IoT becomes a feasible internetworking substrate on top of which M3 spaces can be deployed (Korzun, Balandin, & Gurtov, 2013; Kiljander et al., 2014; Balandina, Balandin, Koucheryavy, & Mouromtsev, 2015; Roffia et al., 2016). Autonomous everyday objects, being augmented with sensing, processing, and network capabilities, are transformed into smart objects that understand and react to their environment. It has led recently to revision of application programming techniques and met with new design challenges for development of IoT service infrastructures (Korzun, Kashevnik, Balandin, & Smirnov, 2015; Korzun, Nikolaevskiy, & Gurtov, 2015; Korzun, 2016a).

This chapter sorts out the following design challenges, which smart space deployment and in particular M3 space applications meet in IoT environments.

- **Interoperability:** How to manipulate with information in an open dynamic multi-device environment and to offer services to the users.
- **Information Processing:** How to reason over the information and to construct the services, despite of environment heterogeneity, volatility, and ad-hoc nature.
- **Security and Privacy:** How to provide integrity and confidentiality of processed data and communication as well as authentication of services and users.

We expect that these challenges are most crucial on the recent phase of M3 architecture realization. Other challenges are their instances to certain extent. That is, seamless device integration is connected to interoperability and security, knowledge exchange between services and understanding of the current situation are related to interoperability and information processing.

# BACKGROUND

The advances in IoT technology lead to emergency of IoT environments in various application domains. Let us overview some of the most promising

IoT-enabled domains where M3 spaces can provide a solid base for creating smart services.

## Collaborative Work Environments

Progressing IoT technologies and new generation of IoT devices make the essential application interest in such a domain as collaborative work, e.g., see (Balandin, Oliver, & Boldyrev, 2009; Takada, Sakurai, Knauf, & Tsuruta, 2012; Korzun, 2016b). In particular, the SmartRoom system is a collaborative work environment for holding conferences and meetings (Korzun, Galov, Kashevnik, & Balandin, 2014). This use case allows enhancing to e-Tourism services when participants collaborate to achieve better cultural experience (Vdovenko, Marchenkov, & Korzun, 2015).

In the IoT-enabled collaborative work environment people can communicate with others for working together, provide own resources to the collective solving process, and access assisting information services. In particular, SmartRoom system provides information services and their visualization to assist such collaborative activity as conferences and meetings in a multi-media equipped room. In the basic scenario, Presentation-service displays multimedia presentations on one public screen in the room (e.g., using a projector) and operates with the related content shared the SmartRoom space. Conference-service dynamically maintains the activity program (i.e., conference section or agenda of talks), which is visualized by Agenda-service on another public screen in the room. Both public screens can be used to show augmented information, e.g., online discussion of the participants during the talk. Any participating user can also access the services using SmartRoom client on the personal mobile device.

The SmartRoom system also serves as base for e-Tourism information systems enhanced with abilities of collaborative work. In addition to individual interactions of end-users with information e-Tourism services, multiple end-users collaborate in the same IoT environment to advance their cultural knowledge. In particular, one scenario for SmartRoom participants is collaborative construction of the social program. The latter includes points of interests (POIs), which a participant can visit during the social event. The organizers provide predefined POIs (e.g., a preliminary tour plan). Then a participant can make own decisions: which POIs are of personal interest as well as preferred time of the visit. This decision-making process is iterative: a participant updates her/his decision depending on observable plans of others. Based on the collected decisions, the organizers then finalize the social program.

## Cultural Heritage Areas

The cultural heritage domain represents a rich resource appearing in both physical and information worlds (Kuflik, Wecker, Lanir, & Stock, 2015). Within the IoT environment, people equipped with mobile devices can interact with cultural objects, sharing and producing data (Chianese & Piccialli, 2014). They are interested in information services to enhance the quality of their cultural experience (Korzun, Varfolomeyev, Yalovitsyna, & Volokhova, 2017).

Many museums have already benefited from "digitalization" based on information and communication technology (ICT). A traditional way for the digitalization is deploying a database or even a museum information system (MIS). Such a system is typically used as an electronic archive or catalogue to collect description for all exhibits (cultural heritage objects). Basic search functions become available for museum personnel to read the collected descriptions as fixed records. The collection storage and management functions in MIS are also performed by museum professionals.

Museum visitors cannot directly operate with MIS or its access is very limited. Fortunately, the progress in IoT technology has already leaded that some museums provide exhibits equipped with IoT-enabled digital equipment. An exhibit becomes able to describe itself to nearby visitors. Exhibits are transformed into IoT smart objects, where such an object is defined as acting autonomously to make own decisions, sensing the environment, communicating with other objects, accessing resources of the existing Internet, and interacting with human. Each can provide on-site personalized services for museum visitors equipped with personal mobile devices. Museum information services are not limited with local description of a given exhibit. They can take into account additional historical sources to semantically enrich descriptions in the museum exhibit collection. The sources can be from exhibits in the local surrounding and from the global Internet as well as from museum visitors and professionals. In particular, a user can provide own annotations and digital pictures for informational augmentation of observed exhibits. That is, in a smart museum, its end-users are explicitly involved in the process of knowledge use and creation.

The use of IoT-enabled location-based services makes possible shortening the information distance between objects in cultural spaces and their visitors.

Rethinking of cultural spaces (from the point of view of their design and services they can provide) for improving visitors experience and cultural knowledge diffusion through IoT has been already started. Based on IoT-enabled sensors deployed in the cultural space, any object can be "dressed" of its context and juxtaposed into it. The sensors observe the environment and support the people enjoyment process, establishing multiple connections among the end-users through which convey information, stories and multimedia content.

The idealistic case, when each museum exhibit is transformed to a full-valued decision-making entity in the IoT sense, is still far from the today's reality. Moreover, some exhibits are non-physical but informational objects (e.g., a photo or audio interview). New concepts for smart museum appear, which involves both physical and information exhibits. The smart spaces paradigm can be used to transform a museum to a collaborative work environment where cultural heritage knowledge becomes usable and creatable by visitors and professionals themselves.

Museum services are not limited with local description of a given exhibit. They become services of high intelligence level since they are able to take into account additional historical sources to semantically enrich the museum exhibit descriptions collection. The sources are from MIS, from exhibits themselves as well as from museum visitors and professionals. A smart museum becomes a service-oriented system constructed on the top of MIS and augmented with other information sources. Importantly that it can access local non-MIS resources from the local surrounding (e.g., from museum visitors and personnel) and from the global Internet. The users are explicitly involved in the process of knowledge use and creation, as it happens in social self-adaptive applications. The system can interact with users through devices sensitive to the environment (e.g., mobile phones).

## Historical e-Tourism

A particular application class for cultural heritage domain is e-Tourism services (Smirnov, Shilov, Kashevnik, & Ponomarev, 2017). An example for history-oriented tourists is the smart mobile assistant that provides personalized recommendations on historical objects as well as their historical relations on the worldwide scale level (Petrina, Korzun, Varfolomeyev, & Ivanovs, 2016). An information service makes automated construction of a personal semantic network from available information fragments. The network is created around a given point of interests (POI) and represents the links between the given POI and other objects (other POIs, persons, and events). The semantic network is analyzed and derived knowledge (e.g., the most interesting POIs nearby) are visually presented to the tourist for interpretation and decision-making.

Historical tourism has distinctive features compared with the general application domain of cultural heritage tourism. The latter embraces both historical and present-day cultural phenomena. Historical tourism addresses the so-called "sites of memory". They present any material traces of historical events, which sometimes coincide with cultural heritage artifacts. For instance, an architectural monument is directly "involved" in historical developments related to its construction. Another example is any place or a spot associated with a historical event. Traces of historical facts are presented in the multitude of historical sources, including open sources in the Internet.

In general, a point of interest (or attraction) is an actual spot with precise localization on the geographical map (e.g., geo-position coordinates or postal address). Nowadays, POI recommender systems form an important services class in e-Tourism (Borras, Moreno, & Valls, 2014; Gavalas, Konstantopoulos, Mastakas, & Pantziou, 2014). In addition to POIs, historical tourism takes into consideration a lot of other historical-valued objects such as persons, events, and data sources (written records and narratives, artifacts, alternative information sources, data and knowledge bases available on the Web, etc.). Relations between historical objects define important semantics. Moreover, any historical event might be conditionally defined as a semantic relation between several historical objects. Ontologies become of high application interest for knowledge representation and reasoning in historical research and e-Tourism.

In historical tourism, we expect that semantic relations can be effectively represented and manipulated using the technologies of the Semantic Web. To the best of our knowledge, no specialized knowledge base that comprise semantically enriched information about historical objects has been created yet. To a certain extent, a corpus of historical information is represented in the ontological form in such knowledge bases for cultural heritage as DBpedia, Freebase, or YAGO. Additional information can be extracted from web publications of historical sources. In these settings, the methods of web-based systems, mobile programming, and multi-agent systems provide effective means for implementation of data search, access, and reasoning.

Semantic Web methods and technologies help to solve the problems of creation, design, enrichment, editing, retrieval, analysis and presentation of historical information. There are mobile services for cultural heritage e-Tourism developed using semantic technologies. For instance, the intelligent tourist guide utilizes cultural heritage information. Nevertheless, the present-day application developments do not take into account the principal peculiarity of historical tourism—semantic relations among historical data. The problem of the semantic-aware retrieval information from multiple data sources can be settled by using semantic technologies, e.g., by parsing the query and ranking the relevance of content. However, effective POI ranking requires the combination of different algorithms. One of the ranking parameters can be the recalls of the users with similar interests that have been posted on the Smart Tourism Website. In addition to users recalls, other parameters should be taken into account, e.g., such context attributes of visited places as time and weather.

## Mobile Health

The traditional style of health monitoring and healthcare by visiting a hospital or clinic to meet a doctor is still the most popular, especially in developing countries. Although a medical information system (MIS) can provide effective digital service support, this form of medical operation is expensive. To make healthcare more effective, continuous health monitoring and use personal analysis of the critical health parameters can be established for the remote patients. This demand drives the development of new approach to healthcare called mobile health or mHealth (Tachakra, Wang, Istepanian, Song, 2003).

An mHealth system is responsible to support and provision of healthcare services using mobile communication devices, such as smartphones and tablets. Mobile devices are primarily responsible for collecting various health parameters data, delivery of healthcare information to medical personnel and patients, online monitoring of patient vital signs, and direct provision of healthcare services. In fact, an mHealth system makes remote users virtually closer to healthcare backend services (located in an existing MIS), e.g., as if the user is located in the hospital.

The IoT concept defines ubiquitous connectivity of a multitude of "things" in the physical surroundings of our everyday life. Basically, the IoT technology provides a way (an infrastructure and supporting mechanisms) to uniquely identify and link objects from out physical surrounding to their virtual (information) representations in the global Internet. Some of these objects can represent medical equipment such as sensors in the user's personal and body area networks. Actions on physical objects and their resources can be replaced by operations on the virtual reflections, leading to a new approach to development of healthcare services (Islam, Kwak, Kabir, Hossain, & Kwak, 2015; Balandina, Balandin, Koucheryavy, & Mouromtsev, 2015).

The classic style of healthcare is limited by the time and space barriers, and a patient always has to visit a doctor in hospital or clinic. Information and communication technologies (ICT) provide a powerful tool to break these barriers. Traditional healthcare systems provide backend services located in medical facility. Such a system is enhanced with information services consumed remotely by mobile patients and medical personnel. Consider the following existing application concepts for the use of ICT in healthcare and well-being services provision.

- **eHealth (Electronic Health):** Healthcare is supported by digital services that are constructed using electronic processes and communication.
- **Telemedicine:** A form of eHealth to provide clinical healthcare at a distance, including physical and psychological diagnosis based on telemonitoring of patients functions.
- **mHealth (Mobile Health):** Personal mobile devices are used for continuous collecting, aggregating and analysis of patient-level health data. On the one hand, services provide healthcare information to medical personnel as well as to the patients. On the other hand, direct provision of healthcare services can be performed using mobile telemedicine.
- **Cybermedicine:** The Internet is used to deliver healthcare services, such as medical consultations, diagnosis, and prescriptions. Services allow patients online access to consultations and treatment with medical professional.

As in many other application domains, IoT can enable healthcare using fusion of real (physical) and virtual (information) worlds (Korzun, 2017). This fusion supports a new level of interconnection and convergence of service-oriented information coming from both worlds (Copetti, Leite, Loques, & Neves, 2013). Healthcare services are constructed within IoT environments. Such an environment is associated with a physical spatial-restricted place equipped with and consisting of a variety of devices. In addition to local networking, the environment has access to the global Internet with its diversity of services and resources, including traditional medical information systems.

Evolving from the world of embedded electronic devices, an IoT environment includes many mobile participants; each act as an autonomous decision-making entity. Furthermore, an IoT environment can be non-fixed: the environment is formed ad-hoc or occasionally (e.g., when some users appear) in a spatial area or the environment is mobile (e.g., around the user) to make a user-centric system accompanying the user.

## Industrial Internet of Things

IoT is making a rapid progress in the Internet by providing connectivity to consumer devices such as toasters to enable their remote monitoring and integrated smart-home solutions. On the industrial side, such approach is referred to as Machine-to-machine or Machine-type Communication, with latest support in ETSI standards. However, the Internet economics presently revolves around mining user data and providing targeted advertisement by giant companies including Google and Facebook. Thus, the best minds in network applications are focusing on creating the best algorithms to overcome ad blocking software and sell something to the users. Industrial Internet aims at changing the game by focusing the talents on data science application to design algorithms to predict machine maintenance needs and streamline operations based on machine sensor output.

The Industrial Internet is a novel concept introduced by General Electric in 2014. Therefore, there is not a lot of research literature on this subject and conferences in this area just start to appear. However, industrial automation is a mature area focusing on connectivity of cyber-physical systems such as Supervisory Control and Data Acquisition (SCADA) and Process Control Systems (PCS).

The term IoT was initially proposed to refer to uniquely identifiable interoperable connected objects with radio-frequency identification (RFID) technology. Now the most common view of IoT refers to a giant dynamic global network infrastructure for the ubiquitous connection of numerous physical objects (e.g., everyday things equipped with RFIDs, various sensors and actuators, embedded and mobile electronic devices, low capacity and powerful computers) that rely on advanced communication and information processing technologies. IoT aims at fusion of real (physical) and virtual (information) worlds, and the IoT concept evolves to service-oriented information interconnection and convergence.

IoT is expected to offer effective solutions to transform the operation and role of many industrial systems (Xu, He, & Li, 2014). This expectation leaded to the concept of Industrial Internet of Things (IIoT) or Industrial Internet for short. Similar ideas are also developed under such names as Smart Industry, Smart Factories, Advanced Manufacturing, Cyber-Physical Systems (CPS), and Industry 4.0 (the fourth industrial revolution). In particular, a CPS is composed of physical entities such as mechanisms controlled or monitored by computer-based algorithms. A CPS creates virtual counterparts to physical components, acting in the networked system as smart objects, similarly to the IoT vision.

Although IIoT applications are still in the early stage, several pilot prototypes are being developed and even experimentally deployed in various industries. Examples include healthcare service industry (Domingo, 2012), transportation and logistics (Karakostas, 2013), food supply chains (Pang, Chen, Han, & Zheng, 2015), and building automation (Han, Lee, & Crespi, 2014). The basic goals that an Industrial Internet System (IIS) should support are: a) increasing the productivity, b) reducing the process maintenance costs, c) providing safety for personnel, and d) making the work attractive.

Analyzing existing IIoT applications we define the following characteristic properties of an IIS (Gurtov, Liyanage, & Korzun, 2016).

- **Participation of All Interested Parties:** Any player of application processes (either human or machine) acts as a smart IoT object. Such industrial objects are autonomous; they interact by network i.e., forming a system with massive and cooperative information sharing and processing. A large family of industrial objects is defined by sensors that measured data for process control and actuators that implement decisions coming from process control. The objects are often mobile.
- **Sensing Automation:** System perception based on incoming data flows from many distributed sensors is automated. This property essentially distinguishes the IIoT case from a traditional enterprise automation system. The automated data acquisition aims at making the system of quick response, even when the application processes are highly dynamic and operate in large-scale distributed conditions. As a result, capture of and access to real-time information become facilitated, and all vast edges of an enterprise operate closer to the process control.
- **Big Data Analytics:** Participation of extremely many objects, when each continuously provides sensed data, leads to voluminous collections of raw data. Those need to be operatively processed to provide knowledge for decision-making objects of the control process.

In contrast to traditional enterprise automation systems, this type of information processing becomes service-oriented and involves cloud-based solutions.

- **Control Intelligence:** The traditional approach of solving a global optimization problem for enterprise-level planning and control is not effective in IIoT due to the dynamicity and large-scale. IIS aims at provision of smart services that represent a tool for operative local decision making. A dynamic change does not necessarily lead to recalculation of the global optimal solution, since a rational reaction can be done locally, on the situation. Decision making is not automated in the mechanical sense, when the reaction is fully determined. Instead, recommendations are provided to appropriate participants to assist humans responsible for the control decisions.
- **In-Depth Rather than Traditional Perimeter-Based Security:** Since the traditional firewall and VPN-based security model continues to fail repeatedly resulting into many reported break-ins to industrial network, a novel host-identity based communication architecture is needed to provide safe Industrial Internet.

# DEPLOYMENT AND DESIGN CHALLENGES

## Interoperability

Information available on some devices may be interesting to other devices of the same environment. Furthermore, some devices should communicate with the external world. Currently, the standards for interoperability have been mostly created for single domains or are controlled by a single company. Such domain specific standards pose considerable challenges for IoT devices. The traditional standardization approach cannot achieve the basic IoT property: a device can interoperate with whatever devices accessible at the given time.

The smart spaces paradigm makes clear separation between device, service, and information level interoperability (Kiljander et al., 2014). Device interoperability covers technologies for devices to discover and network with each other. Service interoperability covers technologies for space participants to discover services and use of them. Information interoperability covers technologies and processes for making information available without a need to know interfacing methods of the entity creating or consuming the information.

Application developer uses KP Interface (KPI) for programming KP logic and its interaction with the space by SSAP primitives (Korzun, Lomov, Vanag, Balandin, & Honkola, 2011). The M3 architecture requires that SIB supports a number of solutions for network connectivity, yielding multivendor device interoperability. For Internet communication, SIB supports HTTP and plain TCP/IP. Short-range wireless communications of mobile devices can use such connectivity solutions as Bluetooth or 6LoWPAN. Network on Terminal Architecture (NoTA) provides a possible solution for embedded devices. Reliable communication on top of IPv4 and IPv6 uses Host Identity Protocol, which supports mobility and multi-homing. Application code developer selects a connectivity mechanism for a device family.

The device heterogeneity introduces additional difficulty for the KP development. If the hosting device is a computer (i.e., relatively powerful OS and ability to run non-trivial programs), then KP can run directly on the device. The computational resources have to be allocated for KPI (SSAP operations, XML processing, networking), KP logic (written by the developer), and local store (knowledge that KP directly processes), see Figure 1 (a).

Techniques for efficient KP programming for mid-capacity devices (laptops, smartphones, tablets, etc.) and certain embedded devices (with embedded Linux, Contiki, etc.) exist (Ovaska, Cinotti, & Toninelli, 2012). If a device is very primitive (even no operating system, like in a sensor), then hosting a KP on the device is unreasonable or even impossible. In this case, such a device can be attached to the space via a dedicated computer running a gateway KP, see Figure 1 (b). The KP has to transform data between the given data format of satellite device and the ontological representation in the KP local store. For instance, this approach is used for constructing personal smart space in IoT-enabled healthcare applications.

*Figure 1. Typical KP architecture: (a) KP running on a computer, (b) KP serving as a gateway for low-capacity devices*

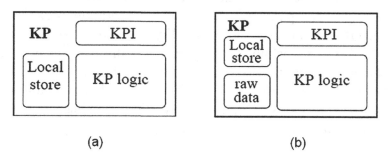

Many of primitive devices are pure data producers in the M3 space. Thus, the required processing at the KP side is small due to the machine-oriented property of RDF. It includes transformation of the raw data into triples and construction of simple SSAP packets in XML or binary format. The above processing can be implemented on the hardware level.

Information sharing in M3 spaces is based on the same mechanisms as in the Semantic Web, thus allowing multidomain applications, where the RDF representation allows easy exchange and linkage of data between different ontologies. It makes cross-domain interoperability straightforward. Application domains are localized, limiting the search extent and ontology governance. That is, for each application its space $S = (I, O)$ is relatively small, allowing computationally reasonable knowledge maintenance at SIB and moderate performance expenses at KP. The interoperability is due to the locally agreed unification of semantics when accessing the same part of the space content $I$. That is, the space-wide ontology $O$ is a virtual application-level component.

The space content $I$ is organized into an RDF graph. Although explicit use of a specific ontology is not demanded, additional semantics are provided by an ontology $O$, usually defined in OWL. For example, a group of KPs can agree an aligned ontology for interpretation of a certain part of the space. The consistency of stored information is not guaranteed; KPs are free to interpret information in whatever way they want. This RDF-based low-level model requires KP code to operate with triples following the SSAP operations directly; the triples are basic exchange elements in communication with the M3 space.

For development efficiency, the high-level ontology-driven KP programming is supported, e.g., SmartSlog SDK. The approach is based on an ontology library, which is automatically generated mapping the ontology to code in a given programming language. The KP logic then is written using high-level ontology entities (classes, relations, individuals). They are implemented with predefined data structures and methods. It essentially simplifies the KP code; the developer has the programming language-like tools to manipulate with the concepts defined in the ontology. The number of domain elements is reduced since an ontology entity consists of many triples. The library API is generic: its syntax does not depend on a particular ontology, ontology-related names do not appear in names of API methods, and ontology entities are used only as arguments.

Notably that ontology library is less machine-dependent than low-level KPI. The same high-level KP code is suitable for different devices since the ontology library can wrap the appropriate KPI (Korzun, Lomov, Vanag, Balandin, & Honkola, 2011).

## Information Processing

The SIB side of M3 space provides mechanisms for knowledge discovery and first-order logic reasoning (Oliver, 2008; D'Elia, Viola, Roffia, & Cinotti, 2015). Each space may contain its own set of reasoning capabilities. The most important mechanisms are semantic queries and subscription (Lomov & Korzun, 2011).

To find appropriate knowledge in $S$ the KP constructs a query using semantic query languages as SPARQL. The SIB resolves the query and returns an ontology instance graph $x \in S$. The KP interprets the result locally and then can insert new knowledge to S or update some previous instances. The appropriate deduction (e.g., deductive closure) is performed by SIB dynamically—at query-time (also at insert-time in some spaces).

A subscription operation is a special case of query—a persistent query, realizing the publish/subscribe communication model in smart spaces. Changes in the space content trigger actions from participating KPs. Subscription is used (i) for synchronizing KP's local knowledge storage with the shared space, as well as (ii) for receiving notifications about recent changes. The latter is a way for a KP to detect events happening in the system.

The RDF-based semi-structured knowledge representation with no strict ontology conformance shifts the responsibility of knowledge interpretation and truth maintenance to the agents. Each KP u manages a non-exclusive part $I_u$ of knowledge and applies own expertise for reasoning over $I_u$. A KP u uses own ontology $O_u$ as an assistance tool that helps to achieve a common understanding with other KPs, see Figure 2. The ontologies and semantic grounding are agreed to ensure a common interpretation and aligned domains. Each KP publishing its shared knowledge provides meta-information to indicate intention for interpretation. Thus, an application is aware of the unification of semantics, which can be done in a localized manner (between a group of KPs) and even runtime. It may result in information inconsistency in the space and misinterpretation on the reader side. The supporting mechanisms to deal with this problem are under development.

The M3 architecture supports multi-space applications when a KP needs the information from several spaces. It provides an opportunity for applications integration in an ad-hoc manner. Notably that the coupling between the

*Figure 2. KPs u and v make own interpretations of the content*

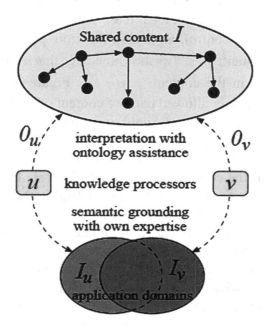

participating KPs is loose and KP granularity can be extremely fine (e.g., a KP can implement a function outside of the hosting UI concept). When an application needs a service from another Smart-M3 application, a KP mediator can be used to connect these spaces. The mediator should properly interpret corresponding knowledge in the source and target spaces, construct a mapping between them, and execute the exchange. Ontology accompanied with logic programming rules can define constraints to which exchanged instances satisfy as well as specify mappings between the spaces.

## Security and Privacy

The security challenge includes traditional issues of open distributed systems, such as key exchange and resource restrictions, and specific problems caused by the dynamicity and heterogeneity of smart spaces. We classify smart space security components onto (a) share level, (b) space access control, and (c) communication. Let u and v be KPs in space $S$.

Security of the share level is based on a sharing function $\sigma_u(S) \subset I$ that defines which locally available knowledge to publish in $S$ for sharing with others. Each KP makes own decisions on its share level, keeping essentially private knowledge at the local storage only. It does not prevent *u* to combine private and shared knowledge in local reasoning.

In the space access control, an access function $\varphi_u$ limits other KPs in access *u*'s shared content; $\varphi_u \subset I$ is the knowledge that *u* allows for *v*. Hence *u* and *v* collaborate in the content $\varphi_u \cup \varphi_v$ as Figure 3 shows. The KPs collaborate accessing only allowed parts of content of each other. Since SIB enforces access control over brokered information, application-specific policies need additional support.

Access control benefits from meta-information published in the space. Exclusive access to the content can be on RDF level. The method allows restricting the access for an arbitrary set of triples. Meta-information is additional triples that specify which data are protected and which KP is their owner. The method may be embedded in middleware data access primitives of a standard KPI, so becoming hidden to the KP developer. Although the method allows extension for more security attributes beside synchronization, any KP is able to see what has been protected in the space.

IoT applications need context-dependent and fine-grained access control. Smart space access control policies define which KPs are allowed to access which objects. Security level of joined devices is measured. An access control ontology allows representing meta-information about the context and granularity. SIB utilizes this information to authorize the access to the space content. The approach enables devices to share knowledge with the same security level even when these devices do not have interoperable security protocols for direct confidential communication. Note that combining security policy rules with reasoning allows exploiting further the advantages of logic programming and description logic. Unfortunately, many reasoning problems in general form require exponential time in the worst case.

*Figure 3. KPs u and v provide restricted content to share in S*

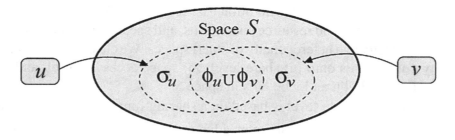

Accessing the space is session-based by join/leave operations. It forms a base for mechanisms of access control and secure communication. For instance, KP identity and cryptographic keys can be implemented with Host Identity Protocol (HIP), which is standardized by IETF. The HIP exchange authenticates a KP-to-SIB communication session based on robust identities. They can be used for access control to different parts of the space, implementing the access function $\varphi$. All transferred data are encrypted, so providing confidentiality and message integrity in communication with SIB. The same approach was discussed in for Transport Layer Security (TLS) protocol. However, TLS does not support mobility and multi-homing as well as causes significant overhead.

Many IoT devices are of low capacity (memory, CPU, battery, etc.), and they cannot use the full scale of security capabilities that the basic HIP or other Internet protocols provide. A HIP-based extension for secure transfer of private data in M3 spaces is proposed in for healthcare applications with wearable and implantable medical devices. The proposal employs HIP Diet Exchange (DEX) to establish secure associations between KP and SIB. HIP DEX requires rather limited computation capabilities from the devices since it uses elliptic curve cryptography to distribute the shared secret. Although HIP DEX is designed for resource-restricted devices it still provides possibility to control performance level by adjusting cryptographic computation difficulty.

## M3 SEMANTIC INFORMATION BROKERS

The central component of the M3 architecture is Semantic Information Broker (SIB). Each SIB manages and shares a knowledge base (KB) with all the smart space participants. The KB is semantic, in the form of a RDF triplestore. Starting from 2008, when the first SIB prototype was produced, several SIB implementations have been appeared optimized for a specific purpose like portability and performance (Viola, D'Elia, Korzun, Galov, Kashevnik, & Balandin, 2016). There are the five open source projects: Piglet-based SIB, its optimized descendant RedSIB, OSGi SIB for Java-based systems, pySIB for embedded and resources constrained devices with Python, and CuteSIB for Qt crossplatform device family. There are also the two SIB designs with no open source implementations: RIBS for embedded devices and ADK SIB built upon the OSGi framework and integrated in the Eclipse Integrated Development Environment. Recently the open source SIB development is supported mainly under the umbrella of the FRUCT Association by efforts of University of Bologna (Italy) and Petrozavodsk State University (Russia).

From a functional point of view, SIB implements an information hub forming a logical rendezvous and information-level interoperability infrastructure on the top of an RDF triple-store (or a SPARQL endpoint). Each SIB acts as an access point to a shared KB that describes the overall information state and context of the environment. The information representation is semantic, based on an oriented labeled graph, i.e., following the SW concept. The basic SIB role is to manage the read&write accesses to this graph. Advanced access operations are possible, including such persistent queries as subscription: a subscription notification mechanism to improve the reactivity and the band usage where the subscribe-notify paradigm is applicable.

The generic SIB architecture is shown in Figure 4. It consists of several modules: network handler, request/response handler, operations handler and RDF triplestore. Network handler implements network communication between SIB and KPs. They exchange messages, which follows the SSAP rules and syntax, recently has being generalized to Knowledge Sharing Protocol (KSP). The SSAP is a communication protocol acting at application level and for which it exists a well supported encoding in XML and a younger, less supported, but thinner JSON serialization. Request/response handler process network messages according to SSAP/KSP protocol rules and syntax and

*Figure 4. Architecture of general SIB*

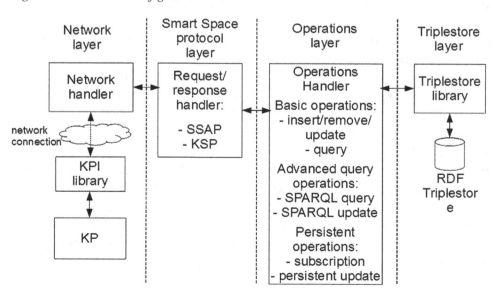

determines which operations should be performed in triplestore. Protocols provides read-write operations for inserting, removing, updating, querying, and (un)subscribing. The set of operations can be extended with advanced SPARQL queries and persistent operations. Operations are performed in operation handlers using a particular triplestore library to manage information in the RDF triplestore.

## The Piglet-Based SIB

The piglet-based SIB architecture is shown in Figure 5 (Honkola, Laine, Brown, & Tyrkko, 2010). SIB consists of two main parts: the SIB daemon (sibd application written in C language with Glib library) and network handlers. SIB daemon handles the information access, operations processing and the storage of the RDF Graph. Network handlers maintain network communication with KPs. The Piglet SIB supports two communication technologies: TCP/IP and Nota implemented as separate applications (sib-tcp and sib-nota respectively). They are connected to the SIB daemon over D-Bus.

The architecture offered the opportunity to add new interfaces by implementing the corresponding daemons and connecting them to the D-Bus. The principles guiding the design of Smart-M3 are simplicity, extensibility and being agnostic to the used communication mechanisms.

The simplicity ensures scalability for small devices and for large number of users, while the extensibility makes it possible to tailor the implementation easily to uses where the standard functionality is not sufficient. Furthermore,

*Figure 5. The piglet-based SIB architecture*

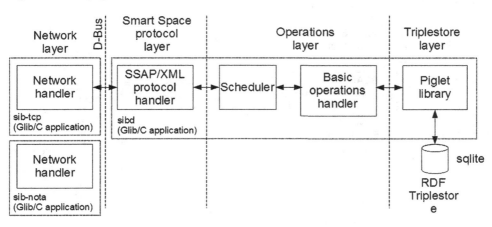

by not dictating a specific communication mechanism, the Piglet SIB should be easy to deployed on top of many existing infrastructures.

The layer runs in a single thread which schedules and executes the requests from the threads handling the SSAP operations. The communication between the SSAP operations threads is handled by using asynchronous queues. The triple operations layer is currently implemented by using Piglet RDF store. The triple operations layer is not tied to any specific RDF store, and any RDF store supporting the basic operations of read, write and delete may be substituted in the place of Piglet. However, changing the RDF store will require changing the code in the graph operations layer to adapt to the concrete interface provided by the new RDF store.

## RedSIB

RedSIB is a direct descendant of the Piglet SIB implementation (Morandi, Roffia, D'Elia, Vergari, & Cinotti, 2012). They share the same architectural design and the code is essentially inherited. RedSIB was built upon the experiences gained in the early Smart-M3 applications. The goal was to solve the most relevant issues the application developers detected as well as improving the performance and avoiding criticalities. Feedbacks of the Smart-M3 community were used to improve the SIB adding more functionalities.

At a high level of the abstraction, the RedSIB architecture (Figure 6) is the same of the piglet-based SIB implementation with one RDF store and two main daemons communicating through D-Bus: the monolithic SIB daemon (redsibd application) and the TCP one (sib-tcp application). A deepened

*Figure 6. The RedSIB architecture*

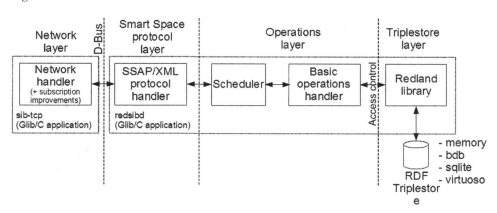

analysis highlights the presence of a high quantity of new code and data structures whose main functionalities are summarized, but not limited to, the following points.

- Support for Virtuoso and for volatile storage (previously supporting only the BDB RDF store).
- Prototype of data access control mechanism.
- Optimization of the subscription handling with several improvements acting specifically for those situations that were considered most common by the community: shortly many subscriptions with low number of triples to be notified at a time.
- Management of the situation of abrupt disconnection happening when a subscribed KP temporarily loose connectivity and the SIB has internal bounds to the active subscriptions.

## OSGi SIB

The OSGi SIB was created and is currently maintained by the University of Bologna and Eurotech (Manzaroli, Roffia, Cinotti, Ovaska, Azzoni, Nannini, & Mattarozzi, 2010). The focus of the OSGi SIB developers is on the IoT and M2M industrial domains. The main strength of the OSGi SIB is its portability: the Java programming language and the OSGi framework grant the ability to run on different operating systems. The development of the OSGi SIB led to the creation of a specific Android version of the Semantic Information Broker, suitable for mobile devices.

With respect to the other implementations of the SIB, the OSGi SIB introduces a new primitive called Persistent Update (PU): it consists of a SPARQL 1.1 update executed once when the command is issued to the SIB and then acting persistently on the data-store until it is deactivated. Together with the Python lightweight implementation, the OSGi SIB is the only one providing support for the JSON encoding of the SSAP protocol which grants a bandwith usage ranging from the 60% to the 90% of the current XML encoding (still in its early stage). The OSGi SIB also provides support for persistent storage thanks to TDB module of the Jena libraries.

The OSGi SIB is implemented as OSGi Java application and is made of several interacting modules – bundles registered to the OSGi framework (Figure 7).

TCP Bundle is responsible for managing the network connection with KPs. It receives messages from KPs and manages a queue of the requests

*Figure 7. The OSGi SIB architecture*

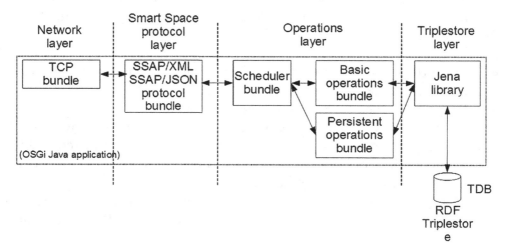

to be satisfied. Protocol bundle parses each message received from the TCP bundle in order to build an internal representation of the request. Scheduler bundle binds an identifier to each request processed by the Protocol bundle and sends request on processing. Operation bundles process each request with help of Jena library and provide a reply. Persistent operations bundle is responsible for the management of every active Persistent Update operation.

## pySIB

Developed by ARCES department of the University of Bologna, pySIB (Viola, D'Elia, Roffia, & Cinotti, 2016) is a lightweight SIB implementation designed to run mainly on embedded devices and System on Chips (SoCs). The implementation is written in Python and relying on the Python bindings of the RDFlib, pySIB results easy to install and run. The pySIB implementation, despite being in its earliest stable releases, shows good performance both in updating the knowledge base and retrieving data from it.

The modular architecture of pySIB makes it easy for the developers to extend it by adding new features or replacing existing modules with different ones (e.g. to support a different SSAP parser). The architecture is represented in Figure 8. The Network handler module constitutes the interface between the SIB and the external world. Every message received from the outside (currently over TCP) is forwarded to the Protocol handler that builds an internal

*Figure 8. The pySIB architecture*

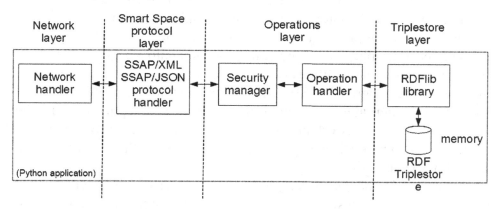

dictionary representation of the SSAP message. The current implementation supports by default the JSON encoded version of the SSAP protocol. Security manager checks access rights on the requested operation and then passes approved operations to Operation handler.

Operation handler performs the actions required by the KP on the RDF store, then sends back a dictionary to the Protocol handler which transform it into a reply message. The Network handler module sends the reply packet to the KP. As triplestore pySIB uses RDFlib library which maintains in-memory volatile triplestore which is fast but not persistent. Due to the modular architecture and to the simplicity of Python, pySIB is also used for educational matters into the Interoperability of Embedded Systems course of the University of Bologna where Smart-M3 has a central role.

## CuteSIB

The CuteSIB implementation (Galov, Lomov, & Korzun, 2015) is developed and maintained by Petrozavodsk State University (PetrSU). CuteSIB is a reengineered version of RedSIB. The implementation is based on the Qt framework in order to support a wide spectrum of Qt-based IoT devices. A modular SIB design was proposed to support such important properties as extensibility, dependability, and portability.

The first distinctive property is elimination of D-Bus. One reason is that D-Bus is used only in Unix-based systems, thus preventing the use of SIB in other operating systems (e.g., Windows). Another reason is that D-Bus does not effectively support transfer of big amounts of data. Operation becomes unstable when transferring fast data streams of triples. As a result of the D-Bus elimination, the interprocess communication has simpler structure.

SIB communication modules for various network protocols (e.g., TCP or UDP) become plug-ins. They can be loaded/unloaded from the main SIB program as dynamic libraries. When higher portability is needed, such plug-ins can be integrated to SIB using static compilation. In this case, SIB does not load external libraries and is used as monolith application with the customizable set of network protocols. This feature targets SIB portability, taking into account devices with operating systems that have limited or no support of dynamic libraries.

The second distinctive property is the plug-ins based architecture in order to achieve higher extensibility due to the modular approach, see Figure 9. The architecture allows inclusion/exclusion of certain modules in compilation phase or in runtime. The feature affords to customize the SIB functionality for given host device and IoT environment.

Network layer is implemented as a pool of access points, each is an external module for SIB. Protocol manager interacts with a specific access point and performs request parsing and response generation.

Access protocol (such as SSAP or KSP) is implemented as a separate module, which parses request messages and creates response messages. In particular, it becomes possible to implement SPARQL over HTTP to

*Figure 9. The CuteSIB architecture*

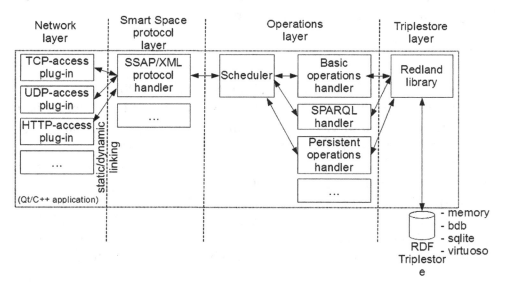

access SIB as a common SPARQL access point. Scheduler module controls processing of CuteSIB commands with KPs requests/responses and internal notifications (to control runtime of other modules).

The scheduler delegates each command to an appropriate operation handler. Three command handlers can be distinguished: basic operation handler (for insert, remove, update, and query operations), persistent operations handler contains persistent operations (such as subscription), and SPARQL handler for advanced search queries. Persistent operations are always stored on the SIB side (continuous in time) and a response is generated whenever a specified event occurs.

## RIBS and ADK SIB

Let us consider two SIB designs that had reached a considerable level of interest in the past, when the Smart-M3 platform was introduced. Although these SIBs have no open source implementation, a summary consideration is still important to contrast the ideas with the other SIB proposals.

The RDF Information Bases Solution (RIBS) is a SIB design with the focus on security aspects and targeted to low-resources devices (Suomalainen, Hyttinen, & Tarvainen, 2010). The prototype unified in a pioneering way two of the main issues that are currently faced by the whole IoT community: the security based on a dynamic set of concurrent policies and the portability on resource-constrained devices. RIBS was born and developed during the SOFIA project (2008-2011) and led to a prototype demonstration in the final event of the project. Despite its good points, being not totally open source, the project failed to build a community of developers large enough to carry the work on after the end of SOFIA. Then, to the best of the authors' knowledge, the development process of RIBS was suspended.

The SIB ADK (Advanced Development Kit) is a SIB version built upon the OSGi framework and integrated in the Eclipse Integrated Development Environment (Gomez-Pimpollo & Otaolea, 2010). It was designed to have a powerful suite for ontology based code generation and model based application development. It is possible to state that the ADK SIB and the frameworks based on it, approach to smart applications in a different but not clashing way with respect to the classical approach matured since the times of the Piglet SIB. Research work and interesting ideas derived from both the approaches and recently it is possible to find also comparison articles (D'Elia, Viola, Roffia, & Cinotti, 2015) even if direct performance comparison is difficult due to the many differences between this specific SIB version and the other described implementations, in particular with regard to the subscription interpretation and management.

## SOLUTIONS AND RECOMMENDATIONS

M3 space applications meet serious challenges when such application targets deployment in IoT environments (). (1) interoperability, (2) information processing, and (3) security and privacy. Table 1 lists the corresponding solutions. Although full-valued solutions are still under development, the presented summary shows the overall feasibility and applicability of the smart spaces computing paradigm for IoT settings.

## FUTURE RESEARCH DIRECTIONS

Knowledge processors running on IoT devices and cooperating in various service scenarios are loosely coupled. The shared content conforms an ontological knowledge representation, supporting also localized agreements and personalization. These properties provide a base to tackle the interoperability challenge.

The semantic reasoning mechanisms and their distributed nature support effective processing within huge multi-source information collections. The M3 architecture states localized ad-hoc spaces and integrates the Semantic Web with other information on surrounding electronic devices. This groundwork feeds and catalyzes solutions to the information processing challenge.

*Table 1. M3 space deployment challenges and their solutions*

| Challenge | Provided Solutions and Feasible Directions |
|---|---|
| Interoperability: device, service, information | Many network protocols. RDF-based operation of SSAP. Multiplatform KPIs and reusable code. Ontology libraries and code generation. Development tools for mid- and low- capacity devices. |
| Information processing | SPARQL queries and first-order reasoning. Subscription and proactive services. Ontology-driven development and runtime mechanisms. Multi-space operation and mediator-based synchronization. |
| Security and Privacy | RDF-based knowledge access control and mutual exclusion. HIP-based network communication. Ontology-based control policies and context-aware security. |

Progress in Internet security protocols provides promising solutions for confidential communications and authentication of the participants with strong cryptographic identities. The computation overhead can be made low, and even low capacity devices are involved into the service infrastructure. Additionally, advanced semantic models equipped with logic programming techniques support fine-grained context-dependent access control to the shared content.

## CONCLUSION

This chapter considered the smart spaces paradigm and its potential for application development in IoT environments. The discussion focused on the design challenges of smart spaces deployment: (1) interoperability, (2) information processing and (3) security and privacy. We provide a systematized view on smart spaces as an effective computing paradigm for IoT-enabled applications in various problem domains. We discussed recent capabilities of the Smart-M3 platform, which provides a promising technology and open source middleware to create smart spaces in accordance with the M3 architecture. The Smart-M3 platform is one of the most suggestive examples of applying Semantic Web technologies to the case of emerging IoT environments. We reviewed existing SIB designs and available implementations, discussing their purpose, strengths, and weaknesses.

## REFERENCES

Balandin, S., Oliver, I., & Boldyrev, S. (2009). Distributed Architecture of a Professional Social Network on Top of M3 Smart Space Solution Made in PCs and Mobile Devices Friendly Manner. *Proceedings of Third International Conference on Mobile Ubiquitous Computing, Systems, Services and Technologies* (pp. 318-323). IEEE. doi:10.1109/UBICOMM.2009.21

Balandina, E., Balandin, S., Koucheryavy, Y., & Mouromtsev, D. (2015). IoT Use Cases in Healthcare and Tourism. *Proceedings of IEEE 17th Conference on Business Informatics* (pp. 37-44). IEEE. doi:10.1109/CBI.2015.16

Borras, J., Moreno, A., & Valls, A. (2014). Intelligent tourism recommender systems: A survey. *Expert Systems with Applications, 41*(16), 7370–7389. doi:10.1016/j.eswa.2014.06.007

Bravo, J., Cook, D., & Riva, G. (2016). Ambient intelligence for health environments. *Journal of Biomedical Informatics*, *64*, 207–210. doi:10.1016/j.jbi.2016.10.009 PMID:27769889

Chianese, A., & Piccialli, F. (2014). Designing a smart museum: When cultural heritage joins IoT. *Proceedings of 8th International Conference on Next Generation Mobile Apps, Services and Technologies* (pp. 300-306). IEEE. doi:10.1109/NGMAST.2014.21

Copetti, A., Leite, J. C., Loques, O., & Neves, M. F. (2013). A decision-making mechanism for context inference in pervasive healthcare environments. *Decision Support Systems*, *55*(2), 528–537. doi:10.1016/j.dss.2012.10.010

D'Elia, A., Viola, F., Roffia, L., & Cinotti, T. S. (2015). A Multi-Broker Platform for the Internet of Things. *Proceedings of Internet of Things, Smart Spaces, and Next Generation Networks and Systems: 15th International Conference NEW2AN 2015 and 8th Conference ruSMART 2015, LNCS* (Vol. 9247, pp. 34-46). Springer International Publishing. doi:10.1007/978-3-319-23126-6_4

Domingo, M. C. (2012). An overview of the internet of things for people with disabilities. *Journal of Network and Computer Applications*, *35*(2), 584–596. doi:10.1016/j.jnca.2011.10.015

Galov, I., Lomov, A., & Korzun, D. (2015). Design of Semantic Information Broker for Localized Computing Environments in the Internet of Things. *Proceedings of 17th Conference of Open Innovations Association FRUCT* (pp. 36-43). IEEE. doi:10.1109/FRUCT.2015.7117968

Gavalas, D., Konstantopoulos, C., Mastakas, K., & Pantziou, G. (2014). Mobile recommender systems in tourism. *Journal of Network and Computer Applications*, *39*, 319–333. doi:10.1016/j.jnca.2013.04.006

Gomez-Pimpollo, J., & Otaolea, R. (2010). Smart Objects for Intelligent Applications-ADK. *Proceedings of* IEEE Symposium on Visual Languages and Human-Centric Computing (pp. 267-268). IEEE.

Gurtov, A., Liyanage, M., & Korzun, D. (2016). Secure Communication and Data Processing Challenges in the Industrial Internet. *Baltic Journal of Modern Computing*, *4*(4), 1058–1073. doi:10.22364/bjmc.2016.4.4.28

Han, S., Lee, G., & Crespi, N. (2014). Semantic context-aware service composition for building automation system. *IEEE Transactions on Industrial Informatics*, *10*(1), 752–761. doi:10.1109/TII.2013.2252356

Honkola, J., Laine, H., Brown, R., & Tyrkko, O. (2010). Smart-M3 Information Sharing Platform. *Proceedings of The IEEE symposium on Computers and Communications* (pp. 1041-1046). IEEE. doi:10.1109/ISCC.2010.5546642

Islam, S. R., Kwak, D., Kabir, M. H., Hossain, M., & Kwak, K. S. (2015). The internet of things for health care: A comprehensive survey. *IEEE Access*, *3*, 678–708. doi:10.1109/ACCESS.2015.2437951

Karakostas, B. (2013). A DNS architecture for the internet of things: A case study in transport logistics. *Procedia Computer Science*, *19*, 594–601. doi:10.1016/j.procs.2013.06.079

Kiljander, J., DElia, A., Morandi, F., Hyttinen, P., Takalo-Mattila, J., Ylisaukko-Oja, A., & Cinotti, T. S. et al. (2014). Semantic Interoperability Architecture for Pervasive Computing and Internet of Things. *IEEE Access*, *2*, 856–873. doi:10.1109/ACCESS.2014.2347992

Kortuem, G., Kawsar, F., Sundramoorthy, V., & Fitton, D. (2010). Smart objects as building blocks for the Internet of Things. *IEEE Internet Computing*, *14*(1), 44–51. doi:10.1109/MIC.2009.143

Korzun, D. (2016a). On the Smart Spaces Approach to Semantic-driven Design of Service-oriented Information Systems. *Proceedings of the International Baltic Conference on Databases and Information Systems, CCIS* (Vol. 615, pp. 181-195). Springer International Publishing. doi:10.1007/978-3-319-40180-5_13

Korzun, D. (2016b). Designing Smart Space Based Information Systems: The Case Study of Services for IoT-Enabled Collaborative Work and Cultural Heritage Environments. In G. Arnicans, V. Arnicane, J. Borzovs, & L. Niedrite (Eds.), Databases and Information Systems IX, FAIA (Vol. 291, pp. 183-196). IOS Press.

Korzun, D. (2017). Internet of things meets mobile health systems in smart spaces: An overview. In C. Bhatt, N. Dey, & A. S. Ashour (Eds.), Internet of Things and Big Data Technologies for Next Generation Healthcare, SBD (Vol. 23, pp. 111-129). Springer International Publishing.

Korzun, D., Balandin, S., & Gurtov, A. (2013). Deployment of Smart Spaces in Internet of Things: Overview of the Design Challenges. *Proceedings of Internet of Things, Smart Spaces, and Next Generation Networks and Systems: 13th International Conference NEW2AN 2013 and 5th Conference ruSMART 2013, LNCS* (Vol. 8121, pp. 48-59). Springer.

Korzun, D., Galov, I., Kashevnik, A., & Balandin, S. (2014), Virtual Shared Workspace for Smart Spaces and M3-based Case Study. *Proceedings of 15th Conference of Open Innovations Association FRUCT* (pp. 60-68). IEEE. doi:10.1109/FRUCT.2014.6872437

Korzun, D., Galov, I., & Lomov, A. (2016). Smart Space Deployment in Wireless and Mobile Settings of the Internet of Things. *Proceedings of the 3rd IEEE IDAACS Symposium on Wireless Systems within the IEEE International Conferences on Intelligent Data Acquisition and Advanced Computing Systems: Technology and Applications* (pp. 86-91). IEEE. doi:10.1109/IDAACS-SWS.2016.7805793

Korzun, D., Kashevnik, A., Balandin, S., & Smirnov, A. (2015). The Smart-M3 Platform: Experience of Smart Space Application Development for Internet of Things. *Proceedings of Internet of Things, Smart Spaces, and Next Generation Networks and Systems: 15th International Conference NEW2AN 2015 and 8th Conference ruSMART 2015, LNCS* (Vol. 9247, pp. 56-67). Springer International Publishing.

Korzun, D., Nikolaevskiy, I., & Gurtov, A. (2015). Service Intelligence and Communication Security for Ambient Assisted Living. *International Journal of Embedded and Real-Time Communication Systems, 6*(1), 76–100. doi:10.4018/IJERTCS.2015010104

Korzun, D., Varfolomeyev, A., Yalovitsyna, S., & Volokhova, V. (2017). Semantic infrastructure of a smart museum: Toward making cultural heritage knowledge usable and creatable by visitors and professionals. *Personal and Ubiquitous Computing, 21*(2), 345–354. doi:10.1007/s00779-016-0996-7

Korzun, D. G., Lomov, A. A., Vanag, P. I., Balandin, S. I., & Honkola, J. (2011). Multilingual Ontology Library Generator for Smart-M3 Information Sharing Platform. *International Journal on Advances in Intelligent Systems, 4*(3&4), 68–81.

Kuflik, T., Wecker, A., Lanir, J., & Stock, O. (2015). An integrative framework for extending the boundaries of the museum visit experience: Linking the pre, during and post visit phases. *Information Technology & Tourism, 15*(1), 17–47. doi:10.1007/s40558-014-0018-4

Lomov, A. A., & Korzun, D. G. (2011). Subscription Operation in Smart-M3. *Proceedings of 10th Conference of FRUCT Association* (pp. 83-94). Helsinki, Finland: FRUCT Oy.

Manzaroli, D., Roffia, L., Cinotti, T. S., Ovaska, E., Azzoni, P., Nannini, V., & Mattarozzi, S. (2010). Smart-M3 and OSGi: The interoperability platform. *Proceedings of the IEEE symposium on Computers and Communications* (pp. 1053-1058). IEEE. doi:10.1109/ISCC.2010.5546622

Morandi, F., Roffia, L., D'Elia, A., Vergari, F., & Cinotti, T. S. (2012). RedSib: a Smart-M3 Semantic Information Broker Implementation. *Proceedings of 12th Conference of FRUCT Association* (pp. 86-98). Helsinki, Finland: FRUCT Oy.

Oliver, I. (2008). Towards the Dynamic Semantic Web. *Proceedings of Internet of Things, Smart Spaces, and Next Generation Networking: 8th International Conference NEW2AN 2008 and 1st Conference ruSMART 2008, LNCS* (Vol. 5174, pp. 258-259). Springer. doi:10.1007/978-3-540-85500-2_23

Ovaska, E., Cinotti, T. S., & Toninelli, A. (2012). The Design Principles and Practices of Interoperable Smart Spaces. In X. Liu & Y. Li (Eds.), Advanced Design Approaches to Emerging Software Systems: Principles, Methodologies and Tools (pp. 18–47). Hershey, PA: IGI Global. doi:10.4018/978-1-60960-735-7.ch002

Pang, Z., Chen, Q., Han, W., & Zheng, L. (2015). Value-centric design of the internet-of-things solution for food supply chain: Value creation, sensor portfolio and information fusion. *Information Systems Frontiers, 17*(2), 289–319. doi:10.1007/s10796-012-9374-9

Petrina, O. B., Korzun, D. G., Varfolomeyev, A. G., & Ivanovs, A. (2016). Smart Spaces Based Construction and Personalization of Recommendation Services for Historical e-Tourism. *International Journal on Advances in Intelligent Systems, 9*(1&2), 85–95.

Roffia, L., Morandi, F., Kiljander, J., DElia, A., Vergari, F., Viola, F., & Cinotti, T. S. et al. (2016). A Semantic Publish-Subscribe Architecture for the Internet of Things. *IEEE Internet of Things Journal*, *3*(6), 1274–1296. doi:10.1109/JIOT.2016.2587380

Smirnov, A., Shilov, N., Kashevnik, A., & Ponomarev, A. (2017). Cyber-physical infomobility for tourism application. *International Journal of Information Technology and Management*, *16*(1), 31–52. doi:10.1504/IJITM.2017.080949

Suomalainen, J., Hyttinen, P., & Tarvainen, P. (2010). Secure information sharing between heterogeneous embedded devices. *Proceedings of 4th European Conference on Software Architecture* (pp. 205-212) ACM. doi:10.1145/1842752.1842793

Tachakra, S., Wang, X., Istepanian, R. S., & Song, Y. (2003). Mobile e-health: The unwired evolution of telemedicine. *Telemedicine Journal and e-Health*, *9*(3), 247–257. doi:10.1089/153056203322502632 PMID:14611692

Takada, K., Sakurai, Y., Knauf, R., & Tsuruta, S. (2012). Enriched Cyberspace Through Adaptive Multimedia Utilization for Dependable Remote Collaboration. *IEEE Transactions on Systems, Man, and Cybernetics. Part A, Systems and Humans*, *42*(5), 1026–1039. doi:10.1109/TSMCA.2012.2183588

Vdovenko, A. S., Marchenkov, S. A., & Korzun, D. G. (2015). Enhancing the SmartRoom System with e-Tourism Services. *Proceedings of 17th Conference of Open Innovations Association FRUCT* (pp. 237-246). IEEE. doi:10.1109/FRUCT.2015.7117999

Viola, F., D'Elia, A., Korzun, D., Galov, I., Kashevnik, A., & Balandin, S. (2016). The M3 Architecture for Smart Spaces: Overview of Semantic Information Broker Implementations. *Proceedings of 19th Conference of Open Innovations Association FRUCT* (pp. 264-272). IEEE. doi:10.23919/FRUCT.2016.7892210

Viola, F., D'Elia, A., Roffia, L., & Cinotti, T. S. (2016). A Modular Lightweight Implementation of the Smart-M3 Semantic Information Broker. *Proceedings of 18th Conference of Open Innovations Association and Seminar on Information Security and Protection of Information Technology* (pp. 370-377). IEEE. doi:10.1109/FRUCT-ISPIT.2016.7561552

Xu, L. D., He, W., & Li, S. (2014). Internet of Things in Industries: A Survey. *IEEE Transactions on Industrial Informatics*, *10*(4), 2233–2243. doi:10.1109/TII.2014.2300753

## KEY TERMS AND DEFINITIONS

**Information Processing:** A process of transformation data into information. In the advanced case, such a process is considered as data mining.

**Internet of Things (IoT):** A concept of providing connectivity of "things" in the physical surroundings of our everyday life. IoT makes fusion of real (physical) and virtual (information) worlds, and the IoT concept evolves to service-oriented information interconnection and convergence.

**Interoperability:** The ability of computer systems to exchange data with unambiguous, shared meaning. Semantic interoperability is a requirement to enable machine computable logic, inferencing, knowledge discovery, and data federation between information systems.

**IoT Environment:** Associated with a physical spatial-restricted place equipped with and consisting of a variety of devices. In addition to local networking, the environment has access to the global Internet with its diversity of services and resources. Evolving from the world of embedded electronic devices, an IoT environment includes many mobile participants; each act as an autonomous decision-making entity.

**Privacy:** The relationship between collection and dissemination of data, technology, the public expectation of privacy, and the legal and political issues surrounding them. Privacy concerns exist wherever personally identifiable information or other sensitive information is collected, stored, used, and finally destroyed or deleted.

**Security:** The term means protecting data, such as a database, from destructive forces and from the unwanted actions of unauthorized users.

**Smart Object:** Acting autonomously to make own decisions, sensing the environment, communicating with other objects, accessing resources of the existing Internet, and interacting with human.

# Chapter 4
# Smart–M3 Techniques

## ABSTRACT

*The previous chapters elaborated the design principles that guide the development of smart spaces-based applications using the Smart-M3 platform. The principles aim at such properties for applications as (i) interoperability for a multitude of participated heterogeneous devices, services, and users localized in the physical surrounding and (ii) context-aware, situational, and personalized service construction and delivery. In this chapter, we present selected ontology-oriented modeling techniques for applying the principles. The aspect of shared semantic information management becomes essential for service construction. We describe techniques how implement this management in a smart space. A question of what is a smart service compared with regular service is still debatable. We describe techniques how implement various intelligence attributes in services constructed and delivered in M3 spaces.*

## INTRODUCTION

As we showed in Chapters 2 and 3, the M3 architecture and its open source implementation in the Smart-M3 platform employ such ontology-aware technologies of the Semantic Web as RDF and OWL (Gutierrez, Hurtado, Mendelzon, & Perez, 2011). This chapter elaborates some selected ontology-oriented modeling techniques to management of shared information within a smart space-based application (Korzun, 2016). The techniques show concrete possible directions for applying the proposed design principles, enhancing the principles to an application development methodology.

DOI: 10.4018/978-1-5225-2653-7.ch004

Context awareness is crucial for making services smart (Vasilev, Paramonov, Balandin, Dashkova, & Koucheryavy, 2012; Korzun, Nikolaevskiy, & Gurtov, 2015). In a Smart-M3 based application the context is shared, i.e., accessible and interpretable by required participants (Smirnov, Kashevnik, Shilov, Boldyrev, Balandin, & Oliver, 2009). To achieve the interoperability, the ontology-oriented technique is used (Kiljander et al., 2014). Moreover, the smart space supports virtualization for effective knowledge sharing (Korzun & Balandin, 2014). That is, we consider the smart space as consisting of information objects and semantic relations among them, resulting in knowledge corpus representation in the form of a semantic network. Its basic structure is defined by problem domain and activity ontologies (classes, relations, restrictions). Factual objects in $I$ are represented as instances (OWL individuals) of ontology classes and their object properties represent semantic relations between objects.

Access to the shared information in the smart space is based on requests (or operations). In addition to instant read and write operations, advanced search queries and persistent queries are possible (D'Elia, Honkola, Manzaroli, & Cinotti, 2011; Galov & Korzun, 2014a). In this case, micro virtualization mechanisms can be used (Smirnov, Kashevnik, Shilov, & Teslya, 2013). Virtual private micro smart spaces are built on the combination of the role-based and attribute-based access control models. Roles are assigned dynamically based on the smart space participant's trust level. The role separation allows simplifying policies and makes them human-readable and easy to configure. The trust level calculation is based on the participant's context, which includes identification attributes; location; current date; device type, etc. Access control rules can be used to calculate the trust level, to assign roles based on the trust level, and to grant permissions to the smart space resources.

Smart space deployment becomes a non-trivial problem due to the essential variety of IoT devices (Korzun, Balandin, & Gurtov, 2013). The traditional case, when a data storage is located on a powerful machine, now is not the best solution. Smart space is considered as a very ad-hoc system, when SIB can run on embedded or mobile devices (Korzun, Galov, & Lomov, 2016; Korzun & Balandin, 2016). Furthermore, the SIB functionality is composite, and some modules can be added or removed in customization of the smart space for given IoT environment and the application problem needs (Galov, Lomov, & Korzun, 2015). The same composite property can be implemented by means of Smart-M3 KPs that run on the same machine as their SIB (Galov & Korzun, 2014b).

## BACKGROUND

A smart space-based application is typically multi-domain and integrates different information sources in the same M3 space, following the principles of localization and virtualization (Korzun, Kashevnik, Balandin, & Smirnov, 2015). Effective structural organization of such heterogeneous information is possible using ontologies, as it happens nowadays in many areas of computer and information science. The ontology formally represents knowledge as a set of concepts within a domain, using a shared vocabulary to denote the types, properties, and interrelationships of those concepts. Ontology management techniques cover processes of acquisition, storage, updating, and utilization of ontologies. For the use in a multi-agent system, its ontology is a formal specification of the concepts and relationships in the problem domain which are needed for agents to operate with. For web applications, the Semantic Web introduced the web ontology language (OWL), a knowledge representation language to encode ontologies (Gutierrez, Hurtado, Mendelzon, & Perez, 2011). It is based on description logic, enabling structural knowledge representation and reasoning. The formalism follows an object-oriented model: knowledge is described in terms of individuals (instances), classes (concepts), and properties (roles and attributes).

The following classification of ontologies is known (Smirnov, Pashkin, Chilov, & Levashova, 2005), see Figure 1. Common ontology describes the conceptual notation of base problem domain. Application ontology contains the terms and structure of knowledge from a particular problem domain and use case scenario. Knowledge source ontology represents knowledge the system operates within the common ontology notation. Request ontology defines terms used by a user to request input information in the common ontology notation. There are two types of augment ontologies: (i) domain ontologies (static knowledge about a particular domain) and (ii) tasks and methods ontologies (problem-solving knowledge: how to achieve the goals). Application ontology describes a real-world application domain depending on particular domain and problem. The ontology integrates tasks and methods ontologies with domain ontologies.

This classification provides a convenient hierarchical way for constructing the ontology $O$ for a given M3 space. On the macroscopic view, an M3 space

*Figure 1. Component structure of ontologies in knowledge-based applications*

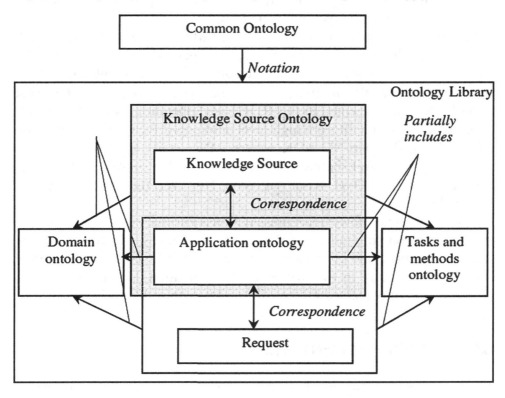

is $S(I,O)$, where $I$ is the content stored in the space and $O$ is the global composite ontology of the application (in the OWL terms, $I$ is an ontology instance graph). When a KP knows $O$ then it can operate with the space content $I$. On the microscopic view, each KP $k$ may have own (small) ontology to operate with a required part $I_k \subset I$. Therefore, M3 space is $S = \left\{ S_k \left( I_k, O_k \right) \right\}$, where $I_k$ are overlapped although $O_k$ may be different. To access $S$ a KP $k$ constructs an ontology-specific query $q(O_k)$. For a read operation, the query returns a subset of $I_k$ for $k$ to interpret the result locally. For a write operation, the query specifies which subset of $I_k$ to replace with given content.

Although ontologies and OWL in particular provide a powerful tool for developers, the OWL syntax is too complicated for machine-based processing. The Semantic Web introduced RDF, a foundation for machine-aware representation and processing of semantic data. On the one hand, RDF provides interoperability between applications, making data interchange machine understandable. On the other hand, RDF supports ontologies and allows extensions with OWL constructions.

Due to this reason, the content $I$ in Smart-M3 is implemented as an RDF triple store (collection of named RDF graphs). Operation of even low-capacity KPs are possible (e.g., sensors and actuators) when they publish/query a small set of RDF triples in a predefined format (a simple ontology). The most of KPI libraries is oriented to this RDF-based operation. Nevertheless, KP development can benefit from high-level ontology-driven code construction using advanced Smart-M3 SDK, where RDF details are hidden and the programmer uses OWL-based constructions. Therefore, development selects between RDF- and OWL-based KP code. However, the same application may include both.

The ontological knowledge representation is a primary tool in the principle of virtualization (digitalization the problem domains and recent system state), in the principle of semantics-aware operation (semantic description and reasoning), and in the principle of information-driven participation (specification of perceived information and recognized knowledge).

## CONTENT REPRESENTATION

The well-known P2P approach can be applied for modeling the virtualization of objects in the smart space and the derived knowledge representation (Korzun & Balandin, 2014). Any object $i$ is treated a peer. Each $i$ keeps some data (values of data properties) and has links to some other objects $j$ (object properties). Therefore, a P2P network $G$ is formed (a semantic network). Contributions from smart space participants (insert, update, delete) change the network of objects, similarly as it happens in P2P due to peers' churn and neighbors selection.

We shall also use the terms a node and a link when referring an element in $G$ and its relation. This P2P model extends the notion of ontology graph (interrelated classes and instances of them) to a dynamic self-organized system. The following model properties clarify this extension.

- **Virtualization:** Objects in $G$ are self-contained pieces of information. It can be effectively described using OWL in terms of individuals and classes. Each object provides a digital representation of a real thing (sensor, phone, person, etc.) or of an artificial entity (event, service, process, etc.). This property suits well the IoT concept as well as its evolution to Internet of Everything (Patouni, Merentitis, Panagiotopoulos, Glentis, & Alonistioti, 2013). Participants (agents) and information objects become equal nodes. From the point of view of applications, all essential system components become observed on "one stage" (with all semantic relations) and manipulated by changing their information representation (digital).

- **Hierarchy:** The decomposition principle from ontological modeling allows defining semantic hierarchies of concepts, e.g., hierarchy of classes of an ontology. Objects in $G$ becomes connected with hierarchical semantic links, as it happens in hierarchical P2P systems. In particular, this technique can be applied for P2P-like structuring personal information about a person and groups of persons (Matuszewski & Balandin, 2007).

- **Emergent Semantics:** There can be non-hierarchical semantic relations in $G$. They reflect the recent state of the dynamic system. For instance, relation "friendship" connects two persons or relation "is reading" appears between a person and a book. Object originals are autonomic and they constantly evolve. The representation of relations between them is also subject to frequent changes. Even global information is highly evolutionary: changes on the object's origin side (not in the representation in $I$) influence the semantics. That is, if an object corresponds to a database then updating its content can change the object's relations to others. This type of dynamic semantics consolidation from the local semantics held by participating objects follows the emergent semantics approach for knowledge management (Aiello, Catarci, Ceravolo, Damiani, Scannapieco, & Viviani, 2008). The property corresponds to the P2P network topology maintenance problem.

- **Composition:** The granularity level of objects provides an additional degree of freedom. One can consider a group of objects in $I$ as a node in $G$ a self-contained element with own semantic relations. For instance, a group of persons forms a team or a service is constructed as a chain of simpler services. From the P2P point of view, the composition property is similar to peer clustering and aggregation, including superpeer-based P2P systems.

- **Data Integration:** A smart space can be considered a virtual data integration system for multiple sources (Bertossi & Bravo, 2005).

Some objects in I represent external data sources (e.g., databases) and the means to access data (or even reason knowledge over these data) from the sources. This property is conceptually close to hybrid P2P architectures and P2P-based search problem, including semantic-aware P2P systems.

In summary, the model allows considering content *I* as interacting objects, which are active entities (make actions) on one hand and are subject to information changes (actions consequence) on the other hand. Result of interaction is derived knowledge in a graph-based form. This fact allows describing formally the conceptual processes of service construction and delivery (Korzun, 2014). Figures 2 and 3 show actions needed for construction of information service and control service, respectively. From the information-centric point of view, we consider a service as knowledge reasoning over the content *I* and delivering the result to the users. Let *o* be a particular ontology used by the service. Write $\left[q(o) \to I\right]$ to denote the action of content retrieval. The result is either existential (yes/no) or constructive (found piece of

*Figure 2. Actions in information service delivery*

**Algorithm:** Information Service

---

**Require:** Ontology $o$ to access information content $I$ of the smart space. The set $U$ of available UI devices.
1: Await $[q_{act}(o) \to I] = $ true {event-based activation}
2: Query $x := [q_{info}(o) \to I]$ {information selection}
3: Select $d \in U$ {target UI devices}
4: Visualization $v_d := v_d + x$ {service delivery}

*Figure 3. Actions in control service delivery*

**Algorithm:** Control Service

---

**Require:** Ontology $o$ to access smart space information content $I$. The set $U$ of available UI devices.
1: Await $[q_{act}(o) \to I] = $ true {event-based activation}
2: Query $x := [q_{info}(o) \to I]$ {information selection}
3: Decide $y := f(x, o)$ {formulation of control action}
4: Update $I := I + y$ {service delivery}

information). Write $I + y$ and $I - y$ to denote the insertion and removal of information piece y, respectively.

The algorithm in Figure 2 embodies actions an information service. Step 1 detects when the service is needed based on the current situation in the smart space. Step 2 makes selection of knowledge x to deliver to the user. Step 3 decides which UI elements are target devices. Step 4 updates recent visualization $v_d$ to include $x$ on device $d$. The algorithm in Figure 3 embodies actions of a control service. Step 1 analyzes the space content to detect that a control action is needed. Steps 2 and 3 are reasoning in context of the current situation, and the service decides what updates (possibly without human intervention) are needed in the recent system state. The updates become available to the participants (original in the physical and information worlds).

## CONTEXT AWARENESS

The context management technique is intended to provide services (constructed in a dynamic environment) with information about current situation, i.e., supporting the principle of information-driven participation (Balandin, Oliver, Boldyrev, Smirnov, Kashevnik, & Shilov, 2010). Two kinds of resources are distinguished in an M3 space: information and acting. The information resources are various kinds of sensors, electronic devices, databases, etc. that provide data & information and perform computations (also referred to as information sources). The acting resources are people, organizations, and electronic devices that can perform certain actions affecting the physical world.

The ontological knowledge representation is used to define a resource behavior model, following the principles of virtualization and of semantic-aware operation. The idea behind the context management technique is to describe this behavior by means of two independent types of reusable components: "domain ontologies" and "task ontologies" (defining domain-independent algorithms that describe abstract methods for achieving solutions to problems occurring in the application domain). The both components constitute the application ontology. This ontology represents non-instantiated knowledge. The components are interrelated in a way that indicates what domain knowledge is used by a certain problem. Context knowledge accumulates up-to-date information from smart space. To take this information into account, the domain and task ontologies have to clearly define the context and related information sources.

Context management technique in the paper is based on knowledge logistics methodology (Smirnov, Pashkin, Chilov, & Levashova, 2005). Context management concerns organization of contextual information for the use in a given application. Context is defined as any information that can be used to characterize the situation of an entity. An entity is a person, place or object that is considered relevant to the interaction between a user and an application, including the user and application themselves. Context is suggested being modeled at two levels: abstract and operational. These levels are represented by abstract and operational contexts, respectively (see Figure 4).

*Abstract context* is an ontology-based model integrating information and knowledge relevant to the current problem situation. Such knowledge is extracted from the application ontology it specifies domain knowledge describing the situation and problems to be solved in this situation. The abstract context reduces the amount of knowledge represented in the application ontology to the knowledge relevant to the current problem situation. In the application ontology, this knowledge is related to the resources via the matching of their descriptions and ontology elements, therefore the abstract context allows the set of resources to be reduced to the resources needed to instantiate knowledge specified in the abstract context. The reduced set of resources is referred to as contextual resources.

*Operational context* is an instantiation of the domain constituent of the abstract context with data provided by the contextual resources. This context reflects any changes in environmental information, so it is a near real-time picture of the current situation. The context embeds the specifications of the problems to be solved. The input parameters of these problems, which

*Figure 4. Abstract and operational contexts*

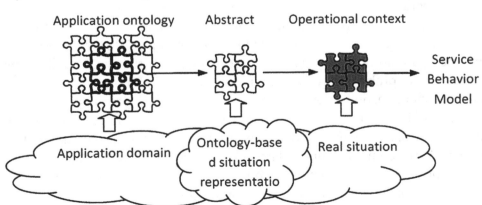

correspond to properties of the classes of the domain constituent, are instantiated.

Constraint satisfaction techniques can be used to take into account dynamic environmental conditions and other possible constraints that have an impact on the problem (Baumgaertel, 2000). These techniques are naturally combined with ontology-based problem definition, and allow setting context parameters so that they would be taken it into account when the current situation constraints are applied. Thus, the problems embedded in the operational context are processed as constraint satisfaction problems in its enumeration form (the result is a behavior model of the smart space service).

Applying these context management techniques to a Smart-M3 application allows to formalize current situation in smart space in two layers and take it into account during application functioning. Abstract context level suits well for sharing and reuse, since, on the one hand, this level does not concentrate on any specific properties, and on the other hand, knowledge of this level is not a universal abstraction rarely taken into account when the case considers practical knowledge sharing and reuse. The KP ontology describe the model of KP and include all requirements and possibilities that can be implemented. Abstract context describes a concrete task that can be solved by a given KP, it is the ontology-based model integrating information and knowledge related to the KP task at the moment.

The model is formed automatically (or reused) applying ontology slicing and merging techniques. The purpose is to collect and integrate knowledge relevant to the current task (situation) into context. Abstract context consists from part of ontology related to this task. Operational context provides description of the task with parameters and values described it at the moment. Operational context is the information that KP publishes in smart space in according with abstract context (Figure 5). A concrete description of the current situation is formed, and the problem at hand is augmented with additional data. On the knowledge representation level, operational context is a set of RDF triples to be added to the M3 space by an appropriate KP. Therefore, others (KP $i$ in Figure 5) can discover these RDF triples and understand the relevant at the moment task. KP $i$ queries information from the smart space in accordance with its task specified in the abstract context. Based on matching of operational context the semantic interoperability is supported. KPs interact in smart space, and then physical devices can implement joint tasks.

*Figure 5. Devices and their services interaction in M3 space*

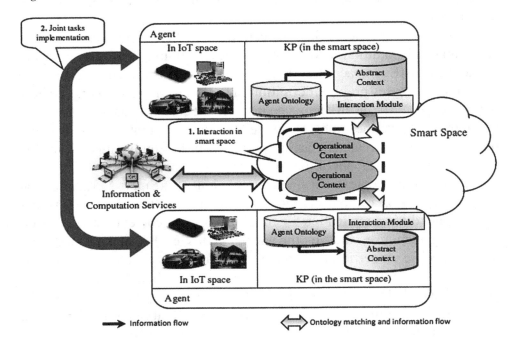

→ **Information flow**    ⟷ Ontology matching and information flow

Semantic interoperability topic covers interaction, knowledge exchange and cooperation between KPs. In a simple case, every KP is constructed on top of common ontology for operation in the M3 space, and the interoperability is straightforward. In certain cases, a joining KP has no knowledge on the right ontology to use. Let us consider a technique that enables KPs to translate between their local and space-relevant ontologies (Smirnov, Kashevnik, Shilov, Balandin, Oliver, & Boldyrev, 2011). The technique supports the principle of information-driven participation (Balandin, Oliver, Boldyrev, Smirnov, Kashevnik, & Shilov, 2010).

When a KP joins an M3 space, the KP should be able to align its local ontology with the right space-specific ontology to operate with the space. A possible solution is that the KP queries (before joining) relevant information units from the M3 space and matches them with its local ontology. In this case, a KP has internal or online accessible thesaurus and implements a mechanism of the ontology matching. The scheme is illustrated in Figure 6. The matching procedure is done "on-the-fly", even if the KP runs on a device with limited resources. Recall that each KP is responsible for certain concrete

*Figure 6. Multi-model technique of on-the-fly matching KP and space ontologies*

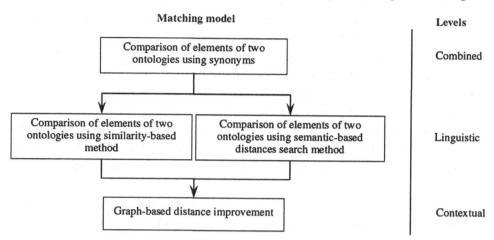

and well-described tasks, i.e., its ontology is typically small-to-medium and describes limited domains.

## ACCESS MANAGEMENT

Initially, the Smart-M3 platform had no mechanisms for access control to information shared in an M3 space (Galov & Korzun, 2014a). However, many applications require possibilities to provide privacy for the user information. In this case, it is needed to provide access control mechanisms for private information of logistics network participants (D'Elia, Honkola, Manzaroli, & Cinotti, 2011). The ontological knowledge representation technique allows to develop the access control model that provides possibilities for content protection and manages access of different KPs (Smirnov, Kashevnik, Shilov, & Teslya, 2013). The model combines the role-based and attribute-based access control models for the access granting decision. The roles are static and set up by an administrator. They are assigned dynamically based on the user trust level and define access rights to the content. The trust level calculation is based on the participant's context, which includes user identification (ID and public key), user location, and current date and time.

An access control broker has been proposed to implement service that is responsible for granting access to the shared content. Protected information is provided only to appropriate participants through temporary private spaces when the corresponding access permissions are granted by the access control broker. This technique provides an example of applying the principle of information-driven participation.

The general access control scheme in M3 space is presented in Figure 7. Architecturally, we distinguish the following components: 1) a participant that consumes the information from the space, 2) a service that produces this information and publishes in the space, and 3) the access control broker that grants access permissions to the participant based on the context. The information flow between the participant and the service becomes private due to the temporal private space, which is physically independent on the public space.

The participant publishes its request to the public smart space for accessing private information and subscribes to the corresponding response. The request initiates the service to query the access control broker. The latter reads the participant's context in the public space and verifies the digital signature

*Figure 7. Context-based access to smart space resources*

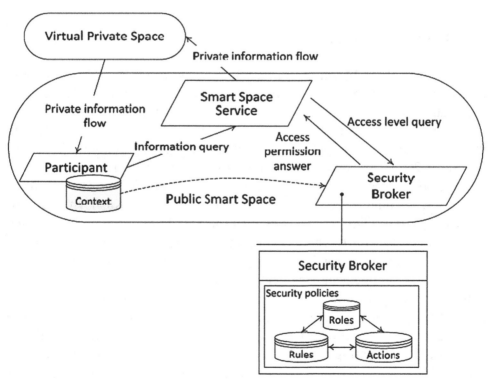

using the open key. If the signature is correct, the broker confirms the user authentication and applies the rules from the security policies (that are set beforehand) to assign the role to the participant. An example of such a rule is constraints for current time like $08:00 < currentTime < 17:00$. A role is assigned to the participants based on the constraints satisfaction assigned for this role.

The access permission is granted based on the role of the participant. For the authenticated participant, the service creates a temporal private space and publishes the required private information there. The space access information (IP address of the SIB, port, and name) is encrypted using the open key and is published in the public smart space. The participant receives the notification by the subscription. If the access is granted the participant decodes the access information with its private key and joins the private smart space. Finally, the private space is removed by the service.

## SMART SPACE DEPLOYMENT OPTIONS

The wireless and mobile settings lead to the following problems that have to be solved in smart space deployment (Korzun, Galov, & Lomov, 2016).

1.  The environment has no powerful server machine locally to host a SIB. Instead, Internet-edge computers such as laptops and various IoT devices are present.
2.  The WLAN has low bandwidth, which is enough to satisfactory serve a moderate number of personal mobile devices with no burst networking activity of their users.
3.  The environment cannot provide efficient access to resources of the global Internet if the transferred data are big and request rate is high.

The first solution direction is to consider SIB deployment in dependence on a hosting computing environment. Importantly that SIB deployment is not limited by a certain class of computing environments, and a smart space can be created in almost any environment with a suitable host device. Furthermore, the emerging concept of edge-centric computing provides many benefits when computations are delegated to Internet-edge devices.

The second solution direction is to add certain service value to the deployed SIB using augmented software running on the same host computer with SIB. The following options are exploited based on the fact that SIB is a middleware system (Galov & Korzun, 2014b).

1. Additional modules are built in SIB.
2. Additional KPs are packaged with SIB.

The first option explicitly advances the SIB with certain knowledge processing functions (e.g., in the form of plugins or added modules). For instance, the CuteSIB design supports built-in reasoning (if needed the appropriate module is added at the SIB compilation phase). Deployed SIB analyzes the collected information and activity of KPs in order to deduce new knowledge. The latter is used by SIB itself for maintaining KPs operation or for enriching the shared knowledge corpus with the deduced knowledge. This kind of knowledge processing is important for system-level tasks such as access control, agent substitution, or subscription notification delivery control.

In the second option, similar knowledge processing functions are delegated to the layers above the SIB layer, as shown in Figure 8. The upper three layers are for KPs in dependence on their role in the applications. KPs on the g-KP layer perform processing useful for many services, even from different domains. Examples include local media-content sharing, local web-page construction, and context-based access control. KPs on the d-KP layer produce

*Figure 8. Service-valued package includes SIB and some infrastructural KPs*

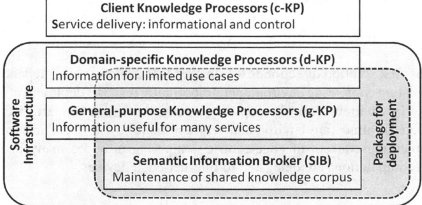

information needed in a limited set of use cases within a certain problem domain. For instance, recommendations construction for e-Tourism domain or monitoring of physiological activity of a mobile user. KPs on the c-KP layer are responsible for service delivery to the end-users. For example, such a KP implements a personal mobile client on the smartphone.

The notion of software infrastructure for a smart space covers all the layers except the c-KP layer. The KPs for packaging with SIB represent a part of the infrastructure that is preferably deployed on the same host computer with the SIB. As a result, the deployed system (SIB plus KPs) can construct services, in contrast to the option of SIB-only deployment. Service delivery to the end-users needs introduction of client KPs, which are not included into the package. Client KPs are installed and run on user interface devices by interested end-users. The packaged system also allows extension with additional infrastructural KPs from the d-KP and g-KP layers, which are not included into the package.

The above discussion showed how the existing consideration of SIB as a pure programming result can be evolved towards packaged software. The proposed deployment solutions aim at configuring the smart space in order to achieve satisfactory performance in the complicated wireless and mobile settings of IoT environments.

To preserve such reasonable performance the application design should take into account that amount of the semantic information needs to be moderate (e.g., several thousands of RDF triples). Non-semantic data must be kept in appropriate databases and information systems, which supports efficient domain-specific methods for data operation. The role of ontology modeling and information-driven algorithms for KPs becomes crucial for semantic linking (not duplication!) all these data sources in the smart space.

Another important performance bottleneck is the wireless network when much data has to be transferred, especially from the global Internet. Since most of such data are non-semantic (e.g., measurements from sensors or media files) this problem can be solved by using variants of local caching and local processing. Our previous work confirms the feasibility of the following solutions to improve the application performance in the wireless network settings.

1. Local web-based content storage.
2. Local dynamic construction of web-pages.
3. Active subscription control from the client side.

From the application design point of view the above solutions shift the workload to the local environment, following the ideas of edge-centric computing. The performance is improved due to eliminating non-local network transfers. The external content is cashed for the local use in domain-specific storages. Moreover, decisions on its processing and integration are also made locally.

In the case of active subscription control, the responsibility is delegated partially to the mobile clients, which are interested in higher performance and ready to spend own resources for this purpose. Therefore, smart space participants have own control on the efficiency of their participation.

## SOLUTIONS AND RECOMMENDATIONS

Table 1 shows possible SIB deployment options in dependence on a hosting computing environment. SIB can be successfully hosted on low-capacity Internet-edge devices if the application does not require much information

*Table 1. SIB deployment options*

| SIB host | Properties | Example Applications |
|---|---|---|
| Local computer | The smart space is used for services accessed within the corporate network. Candidates for the local host are not limited with traditional server machines: a desktop, laptop, or single-board computer (e.g., Raspberry Pi) can be used. | Smart room environments for collaborative work such as SmartRoom (Korzun, Galov, Kashevnik, & Balandin, 2014). Accessing the SIB in WLAN is more efficient when a SIB located on a remote server. |
| WLAN router | A particular case of the local computer option. The smart space is used for services consumed by closely located end-users. Some non-traditional computers of the environment, which are directly involved to the service scenario, can potentially host a SIB (e.g., a media-projector). | Smart room environments with dynamic mobile end-users, embedded devices, and multi-media equipment. For instance, the e-Tourism extension of SmartRoom supports its mobile users to collaboratively construct their trips (Vdovenko, Marchenkov, & Korzun, 2015). |
| Personal mobile computer | The smart space is used for services that accompany the mobile user, exploiting the capacity of her/ his smartphone or tablet. The option advances the standalone mobile application style by making the mobile computer a small local server (which can access external resources from the global Internet). | Personal smart spaces for services that accompany the user. For instance, personalized m-Health system exploits the smartphone to integrate the patient's health parameters monitored by sensors in the personal and body area networks (Korzun, 2017). |
| Internet server | The smart space is used for ubiquitously accessed services, advancing the web-server style of service provision. Although the option supports creating a smart space not associated with a physical spatial-restricted place, the localization is due to the limited set of participants (end-users, devices, or external services). | Mobile smart spaces for services that dynamically involve Internet resources and surrounding equipment. For instance, smart assistant for tourists constructs recommendations on POIs to analyze based on open Internet resources (Petrina, Korzun, Varfolomeyev, & Ivanovs, 2016). |

to dynamically store and process. Since an important performance bottleneck is the network, localized solutions should be used to shift the workload to the local environment, eliminating the need to transfer much data outside the WLAN.

## FUTURE RESEARCH DIRECTIONS

The presented ontology-oriented modeling techniques are in the form of an engineering prototype. For successful practical application more research and development is still needed. In particular, code generation techniques should be used to automatically produce code of KPs based on given ontologies. Effective ontology-driven algorithms should be implemented on the SIB side to support participating KPs with advanced access to the smart space content.

The considered deployment solutions are in the scope of edge-centric computing. The tradeoff how to balance the workload and delegate information processing is still an open issue. In the M3 space case, SIB can be successfully hosted on low-capacity Internet-edge devices if the application does not require much information to dynamically store and process. Similarly, KPs are deployed on available devices of the IoT environment for the given problem domain. Nevertheless, the foundations of this type of deployment and corresponding programming methods are still an open area for research.

## CONCLUSION

This chapter showed that the smart spaces paradigm, the M3 architecture, and its implementation in the Smart-M3 platform provide together an efficient and scalable ground for development of intelligent service-oriented systems as smart spaces-based applications. We showed how the context awareness can be implemented for M3 space applications. We discussed the problems of advanced access to the shared information in M3 spaces. We analyzed the non-trivial problem of smart space deployment in IoT environments. Particular case studies for various problem domains are considered in the next chapter.

# REFERENCES

Aiello, C., Catarci, T., Ceravolo, P., Damiani, E., Scannapieco, M., & Viviani, M. (2008). Emergent semantics in distributed knowledge management. In R. Nayak, N. Ichalkaranje, & L. Jain (Eds.), Evolution of the Web in Artificial Intelligence Environments, SCI (Vol. 130, pp. 201-220). Springer. doi:10.1007/978-3-540-79140-9_9

Balandin, S., Oliver, I., Boldyrev, S., Smirnov, A., Kashevnik, A., & Shilov, N. (2010). Anonymous Agent Coordination in Smart Spaces. *Proceedings of The Fourth International Conference on Mobile Ubiquitous Computing, Systems, Services and Technologies* (pp. 242-246). IARIA.

Baumgaertel, H. (2000). Distributed Constraint Processing for Production Logistics. *IEEE Intelligent Systems, 15*(1), 40–48. doi:10.1109/5254.820328

Bertossi, L., & Bravo, L. (2005). Consistent query answers in virtual data integration systems. In L. Bertossi, A. Hunter, & T. Schaub (Eds.), Inconsistency Tolerance, LNCS (Vol. 3300, pp. 42-83). Springer. doi:10.1007/978-3-540-30597-2_3

D'Elia, A., Honkola, J., Manzaroli, D., & Cinotti, T. S. (2011). Access Control at Triple Level: Specification and Enforcement of a Simple RDF Model to Support Concurrent Applications in Smart Environments. *Proceedings of Internet of Things, Smart Spaces, and Next Generation Networks and Systems: 11th International Conference NEW2AN 2011 and 4th Conference ruSMART 2011, LNCS* (Vol. 6869, pp. 63-74). Springer.

Galov, I., & Korzun, D. (2014a). A Notification Model for Smart-M3 Applications. In S. Balandin, S. Andreev, & Y. Koucheryavy (Eds.), Internet of Things, Smart Spaces, and Next Generation Networks and Systems, LNCS (Vol. 8638, pp. 121-132). Springer. doi:10.1007/978-3-319-10353-2_11

Galov, I., & Korzun, D. (2014b). Fault Tolerance Support of Smart-M3 Application on the Software Infrastructure Level. *Proceedings of 16th Conference of Open Innovations Association FRUCT* (pp. 16-23). IEEE. doi:10.1109/FRUCT.2014.7000926

Galov, I., Lomov, A., & Korzun, D. (2015). Design of Semantic Information Broker for Localized Computing Environments in the Internet of Things. *Proceedings of 17th Conference of Open Innovations Association FRUCT* (pp. 36-43). IEEE. doi:10.1109/FRUCT.2015.7117968

Gutierrez, C., Hurtado, C. A., Mendelzon, A. O., & Perez, J. (2011). Foundations of Semantic Web databases. *Journal of Computer and System Sciences*, *77*(3), 520–541. doi:10.1016/j.jcss.2010.04.009

Kiljander, J., DElia, A., Morandi, F., Hyttinen, P., Takalo-Mattila, J., Ylisaukko-Oja, A., & Cinotti, T. S. et al. (2014). Semantic Interoperability Architecture for Pervasive Computing and Internet of Things. *IEEE Access*, *2*, 856–873. doi:10.1109/ACCESS.2014.2347992

Korzun, D. (2014). Service Formalism and Architectural Abstractions for Smart Space Applications. *Proceedings of the 10th Central and Eastern European Software Engineering Conference in Russia* (pp. 1-7). ACM. doi:10.1145/2687233.2687253

Korzun, D. (2016). On the Smart Spaces Approach to Semantic-driven Design of Service-oriented Information Systems. In *Proceedings of the International Baltic Conference on Databases and Information Systems, CCIS* (Vol. 615, pp. 181-195). Springer International Publishing. doi:10.1007/978-3-319-40180-5_13

Korzun, D. (2017). Internet of things meets mobile health systems in smart spaces: An overview. In C. Bhatt, N. Dey, & A. S. Ashour (Eds.), Internet of Things and Big Data Technologies for Next Generation Healthcare, SBD (Vol. 23, pp. 111-129). Springer International Publishing.

Korzun, D., & Balandin, S. (2014). A Peer-to-Peer Model for Virtualization and Knowledge Sharing in Smart Spaces. *Proceedings of the Eighth International Conference on Mobile Ubiquitous Computing, Systems, Services and Technologies* (pp. 87-92). IARIA.

Korzun, D., & Balandin, S. (2016). Personalizing the Internet of Things Using Mobile Information Services. *Proceedings of The Tenth International Conference on Mobile Ubiquitous Computing, Systems, Services and Technologies* (pp. 184-189). IARIA.

Korzun, D., Balandin, S., & Gurtov, A. (2013). Deployment of Smart Spaces in Internet of Things: Overview of the Design Challenges. *Proceedings of Internet of Things, Smart Spaces, and Next Generation Networks and Systems: 13th International Conference NEW2AN 2013 and 5th Conference ruSMART 2013* (vol. 8121 of Lecture Notes in Computer Science, pp. 48-59). Springer.

Korzun, D., Galov, I., Kashevnik, A., & Balandin, S. (2014), Virtual Shared Workspace for Smart Spaces and M3-based Case Study. *Proceedings of 15th Conference of Open Innovations Association FRUCT* (pp. 60-68). IEEE. doi:10.1109/FRUCT.2014.6872437

Korzun, D., Galov, I., & Lomov, A. (2016). Smart Space Deployment in Wireless and Mobile Settings of the Internet of Things. *Proceedings of the 3rd IEEE IDAACS Symposium on Wireless Systems within the IEEE International Conferences on Intelligent Data Aquisition and Advanced Computing Systems: Technology and Applications* (pp. 86-91). IEEE. doi:10.1109/IDAACS-SWS.2016.7805793

Korzun, D., Kashevnik, A., Balandin, S., & Smirnov, A. (2015). The Smart-M3 Platform: Experience of Smart Space Application Development for Internet of Things. *Proceedings of Internet of Things, Smart Spaces, and Next Generation Networks and Systems: 15th International Conference NEW2AN 2015 and 8th Conference ruSMART 2015, LNCS* (Vol. 9247, pp. 56-67). Springer International Publishing.

Korzun, D., Nikolaevskiy, I., & Gurtov, A. (2015). Service Intelligence and Communication Security for Ambient Assisted Living. *International Journal of Embedded and Real-Time Communication Systems*, 6(1), 76–100. doi:10.4018/IJERTCS.2015010104

Matuszewski, M., & Balandin, S. (2007). Peer-to-peer knowledge sharing in the mobile environment. *Proceedings of 5th International Conference on Creating, Connecting and Collaborating Through Computing* (pp. 76–83). IEEE Computer Society. doi:10.1109/C5.2007.24

Patouni, E., Merentitis, A., Panagiotopoulos, P., Glentis, A., & Alonistioti, N. (2013). Network virtualisation trends: Virtually anything is possible by connecting the unconnected. *Proceedings of IEEE Software Defined Networks for Future Networks and Services* (pp. 1-7). IEEE. doi:10.1109/SDN4FNS.2013.6702545

Petrina, O. B., Korzun, D. G., Varfolomeyev, A. G., & Ivanovs, A. (2016). Smart Spaces Based Construction and Personalization of Recommendation Services for Historical e-Tourism. *International Journal on Advances in Intelligent Systems*, 9(1&2), 85–95.

Smirnov, A., Kashevnik, A., Shilov, N., Balandin, S., Oliver, I., & Boldyrev, S. (2010, October 25-30). On-the-Fly Ontology Matching for Smart M3-based Smart Spaces. *Proc. First Intern. Conf. on Mobile Ubiquitous Computing, Systems, Services and Technologies (UBICOMM 2010)*. Florence, Italy (pp. 225 – 230).

Smirnov, A., Kashevnik, A., Shilov, N., Balandin, S., Oliver, I., & Boldyrev, S. (2011). Principles of Ontology Matching, Translation and Interpretation in Smart Spaces. *Proceedings of IEEE Consumer Communications and Networking Conference* (pp. 158-162). IEEE. doi:10.1109/CCNC.2011.5766443

Smirnov, A., Kashevnik, A., Shilov, N., Boldyrev, S., Balandin, S., & Oliver, I. (2009). Context-Aware Smart Space - Reference Model. *Proceedings of International Conference on Advanced Information Networking and Applications Workshops* (pp. 261-265). IEEE. doi:10.1109/WAINA.2009.104

Smirnov, A., Kashevnik, A., Shilov, N., & Teslya, N. (2013). Context-based access control model for smart space. *Proceedings of 5th International Conference on Cyber Conflict* (pp. 1-15). IEEE.

Smirnov, A., Pashkin, M., Chilov, N., & Levashova, T. (2005). Constraint-driven methodology for context-based decision support. *Journal of Decision Systems*, *14*(3), 279–301. doi:10.3166/jds.14.279-301

Vasilev, A., Paramonov, I., Balandin, S., Dashkova, E., & Koucheryavy, Y. (2012). Context capturing in smart space applications. *Network Protocols and Algorithms*, *4*(4), 84–100. doi:10.5296/npa.v4i4.2169

Vdovenko, A. S., Marchenkov, S. A., & Korzun, D. G. (2015). Enhancing the SmartRoom System with e-Tourism Services. *Proceedings of 17th Conference of Open Innovations Association FRUCT* (pp. 237-246). IEEE. doi:10.1109/FRUCT.2015.7117999

## KEY TERMS AND DEFINITIONS

**Ambient Intelligence (AmI):** Electronic (or digital) environments that are sensitive and responsive to the presence of people.

**Context:** Information about a location, its environmental attributes (e.g., noise level, light intensity, temperature, and motion) and the people, devices, objects and software agents it contains. Context may also include system capabilities, services offered and sought, the activities and tasks in which people and computing entities are engaged, and their situational roles, beliefs, and intentions.

**Edge-Centric Computing:** The paradigm that is pushing the frontier of computing applications, data, and services away from centralized nodes to the logical extremes of a network.

**Knowledge Reasoning:** A process of understanding the given information and extraction (derivation) of new knowledge and facts.

**Ontology:** A formal naming and definition of the types, properties, and interrelationships of the entities that really or fundamentally exist for a particular domain of discourse. An ontology compartmentalizes the variables needed for some set of computations and establishes the relationships between them.

**Packaged Software System:** An organized collection of multiple packages, or a package consisting of multiple separate pieces.

**Semantic Interoperability:** The ability of computer systems to exchange data with unambiguous, shared meaning.

**Smart Space Deployment:** Creating a smart space by running its semantic information broker on a host device of the IoT environment.

# Chapter 5
# Application Case Studies

## ABSTRACT

*The previous chapters showed theoretical foundations and development techniques for the Smart Spaces concept. This chapter presents appraisal of the M3-based smart spaces for Internet of Thing application development. Six topical application domains has been chosen: collaborative work environments, social networking, transport logistics, mobile e-Tourism services, mobile health, and industrial Internet. Existing pilot implementations of applications for these domains show that M3 space is useful for smart services collaboration since it provides possibilities of semantic-based information sharing between services using the publish/subscribe mechanism.*

## INTRODUCTION

Internet of Thinks becomes more and more popular last years it is a paradigm, which supports internetworking of different devices and sensors in the Internet that shown by Gubbi et al. (2013) and Manyika et al. (2015). In according with Atzori et al. (2010) and Wang et al. (2013) the most common view of IoT refers to the connection of physical objects, while the core of technology is in information interconnection and convergence. Producers of home appliances supply devices with Internet access and provides for the market useful smart home-based applications. Internet of Things provides a lot of possibilities for use cases development since a lot of devices and services in the Internet can participate in these scenarios.

DOI: 10.4018/978-1-5225-2653-7.ch005

Recall from the previous chapters that the smart spaces concept, according with Cook et al. (2007), Oliver and Boldyrev (2009), and Gilman et al. (2013), aims at application development for advanced computing environments, when participating objects acquire and apply knowledge for service construction in order to enhance user experience, quality and reliability of the provided information. Each participating object is represented with a software agent—an autonomous information processing unit, which is not necessarily attached to a fixed device say Kortuem et al. (2010). Services are constructed by agents interacting on shared information, i.e., the interaction is indirect and based on publish / subscribe mechanism, in contrast to the communication level provided by the IoT technology. Agents act as knowledge processors to create proper service construction chains. At the end of the chain a meaningful information value is shaped to deliver it as a service to the users.

In this chapter, six topical application domains are considered: collaborative work environments, social networking, transport logistics, mobile e-Tourism services, mobile health, and industrial Internet. Existing pilot implementations of applications for these domains show that M3 space is useful for smart services collaboration since it provides possibilities of semantic-based information sharing between services using the publish / subscribe mechanism.

## BACKGROUND

The main idea of the chapter is showing the applicability of smart space approach for Internet of Things-based applications. The section describes six hot application domains that have been chosen and developed on top of the Smart-M3 platform: collaborative work environments, social networking, transport logistics, mobile e-Tourism services, mobile health, and industrial Internet. The use cases have been developed in the scope of KA179 and KA322 projects of Karelia ENPI programme, which is co-funded by the European Union, the Russian Federation, and the Republic of Finland. For each domain reference model and research prototype system have been developed. They provide substantial evaluation of the smart spaces approach presented in previous chapters.

# COLLABORATIVE WORK ENVIRONMENTS

New generation of personal devices such as smartphone and tablet computer, allows people to effectively communicate with others for working together, to provide own resources to the collective solving process, and access assisting services in the workspace. The SmartRoom system described in details by Korzun et al. (2013). It illustrates the needs of collaborative activity and motivates employing smart spaces for this application class. The SmartRoom system has been approved in several conferences organized by Open Innovations Association FRUCT.

In such activity as conferencing, meetings or seminars, a virtual shared workspace (conference room) can be constructed to support activity operation for local and remote participants. Computing equipment is localized in a room and WLAN provides the network connectivity. Examples of devices are interfaces for media information (e.g., projector–computer pairs, TV panels, interactive boards), sensing devices (e.g., physical sensors and actuators, network activity detectors, microphones, cameras), user access and control devices (e.g., laptops, netbooks, smartphones), WLAN infrastructure (e.g., Wi-Fi access points).

The services simplify organization (e.g., agenda management), material presentation (e.g., slide show), and interactions (e.g., online discussion). Routine procedures of information acquirement, sharing, and transformation are automated. This automated and intelligent assistance allows the participants to concentrate on the problems the activity is devoted to, not on technical details of information acquisition, sharing, and transformation.

The M3 space manages the semantics of the activity, controls the services and surrounding equipment, and relates all information that the activity needs and collaboratively produces. The services are accessible and the activity is controllable from personal devices and room equipment (e.g., whiteboard). The most important information, such as current speaker's presentation and activity agenda, is visualized on big displays.

The reference model of SmartRoom system is shown in Figure. 1. The core KPs are Agenda KP and Presentation KP with appropriate ontologies ($O_A$ and $O_P$). They maintain the activity program and digital presentational content of each speaker, respectively. Two (large) public screens are used as interfaces for these KPs.

*Figure 1. The SmartRoom application architecture*

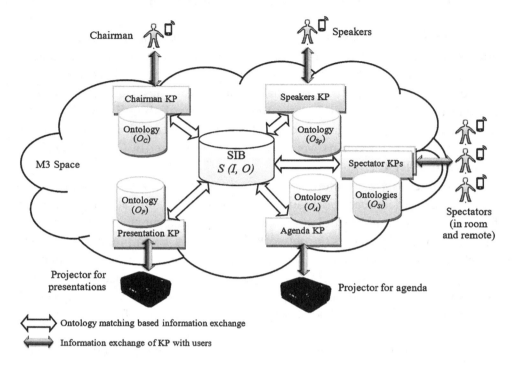

SmartRoom services can be accessed personally using clients (chairman and speaker KPs with appropriate ontologies $O_C$ and $O_{Sp}$). Although all SmartRoom services are potentially applicable for any participant, a specific service subset is offered for each user based on her/his preferences and current context. It aims at personalization and enables proactive delivery of services.

Chairman and speaker KPs are also used for input: users can explicitly or implicitly provide information for sharing in the space. This option implements control actions when ingoing information effects the process (e.g., slide control, changes in the agenda). The SmartRoom M3 space keeps representation of activity processes. Any change in the representation is a control action. Therefore, KPs analyze the online space content, reasons over this information, and updates (possibly without human intervention) the representation. For instance, detection of an absent speaker leads to canceling her/his presentation, recalculating the agenda, and delegating the control on presentation to the next speaker. The organizers (chairman) have full manual control of SmartRoom processes.

Spectators KPs are used to provide an access to SmartRoom services for the activity participants. E.g., when the participants enter to the room, the smartphone connects to smart space and implement ontology matching between Spectator ontology ($O_{Si}$) and M3 information storage ($I$). This procedure allows for the Spectator KP understand what information it can acquire from M3 space and what information it has to publish to M3 space.

The M3 space acts as a hub to relate all data sources and participants. The SmartRoom ontology defines how the data are related to different services and users are represented (Figure 2). It consists of two parts: service ontology and user profile ontology. The service ontology describes a generic service. Each service is represented with the class Service and has such properties as name, description, and status (whether the service is available at the moment or not). The SmartRoom service ontology can be considered as a collection of several subontologies, each aims at a specific service. That is, a KP may operate only within certain subontologies, without the need of understanding the whole system.

*Figure 2. The ontology of the SmartRoom system*

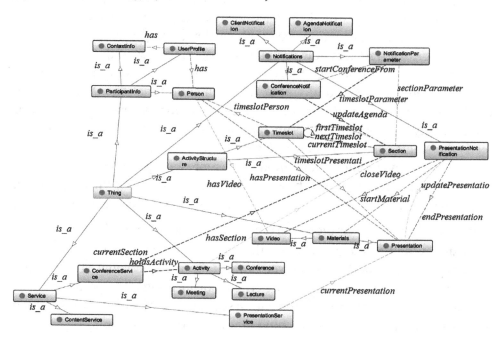

# SOCIAL NETWORKING

Services for social networking have become nowadays of the massive use. The feasibility of applying the M3 concept for construction of proactive, personalized, and composite services for the blogosphere is demonstrated on SmartScribo system that is described in details by Korzun et al. (2012).

In addition to the ubiquitous mobility of users, a challenge, which many social networking applications have already faced with, is that giant data collections are accumulated by a multitude of loosely coupled services. A good example is blogging, where bloggers are mobile and need to permanently operate with many blogs at many blog services (e.g., LiveJournal, Twitter). The physical world introduces the next wave of data sources to appear in blogs.

Although the blogosphere is a huge data pool, a small fraction of the data is needed to any blogger at given time. The smart space can implement a semantic hub that represents this dynamic fraction; it relates the information from multiple blogs from many services and relevant bloggers.

The architectural scheme is shown in Figure 3. The system consists of the following KPs: clients (e.g., Bob and Alice) and blog processors. Clients run on smartphones, operate with blogs locally, share personal data and context of the users, and access the M3 space for operations at blog services. Blog processors connect the smart space with particular blog-services. Basically, a blog processor transfers new or updated blog messages to the blog service and retrieve from the service those blog messages that are of user's current interest. Mediators extend blogging with semantic functions. For instance, in blog recommendation, the blog processor performs search functions of semantically appropriate blogs in the blogosphere, ranks the results, and feeds the smart space with new content for the user.

The high-level ontological model to represent personal and context information and relations with blogs is shown in Figure 4. The virtual personal smart space of a user $u$ keeps content $I_u = \left[ P_u \cup C_u \cup D_u \right]_O$ where $P_u$ is personal data, $C_u$ is context, $D_u$ is blog data (account in a social network). Information consistency and relations between the subsets is ensured by the common ontology $O$. The model allows semantic linking of personal spaces, e.g., representing that some bloggers are friends or forming a temporal group of the mutual interest. In a recommendation scenario, this semantic information allows recommending the same blog messages to several users.

The mediator-based model supports context awareness. A mediator analyzes the context $C_u$ available in the smart space and activates appropriate blog

*Figure 3. The SmartScribo application architecture*

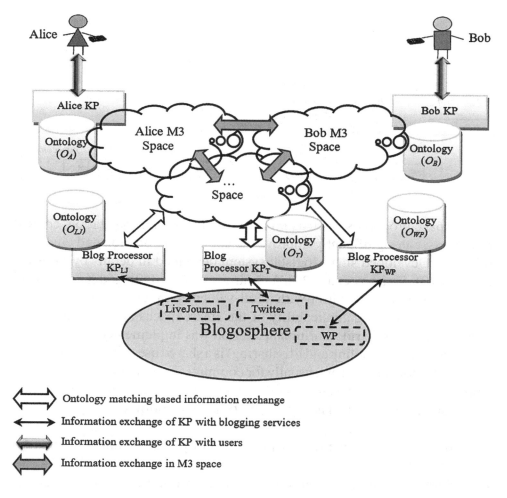

processors and clients using the pub/sub coordination model. In this case, a blog mediator can be associated with a blog search engine (external system).

## TRANSPORT LOGISTICS

Transport logistic is a growing area in the Internet applications market. A lot of goods have to be transported from one place to another every day. People travel around the world and they would like to have a comfortable way for transportation between countries, regions, cities, and locations in one city.

*Figure 4. The ontology of the SmartScribo system*

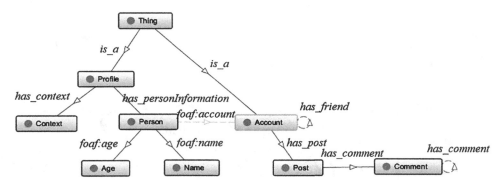

Smart space properties, such as proactive delivery, personalization, context awareness, can significantly improve the application function and quality in this area. Developed smart logistic system described in details by Smirnov et al. (2010), Smirnov et al. (2011), Smirnov et al. (2012), and Kashevnik et al. (2012) can provide a user with a full-valued complex solution.

For demonstrating applicability of the smart spaces approach for smart logistics, a dynamic ridesharing application was implemented. Ridesharing (also known as carpooling and lift-sharing) is a shared use of a car by the driver and one or more passengers, usually for commuting. Dynamic Ridesharing is a ridesharing service that enables a dynamic formation of carpools depending on the current situation. The key properties are as follows.

- Arrangement of one-time trips instead of persistent appointments for commuters.
- Mobile phones are client devices for submitting ridesharing requests and propose offers.
- Automated and instant matching of rides through a dedicated network service.

Ridesharing application consists of drivers & passengers KPs (with appropriate ontologies $O_D$ and $O_p$) and ridesharing broker KP (with ontology $O_B$) (see Figure 5). Driver and passenger KPs collect information about their location, agenda, preferences, and most frequent routes. They implement ontology matching procedure between $O_D$ and $O_p$ ontologies and M3 space content (*I*) The driver or passenger can set additional constraints, for example,

*Figure 5. The dynamic ridesharing application architecture*

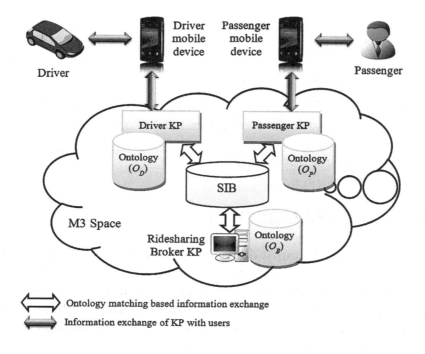

⟺ Ontology matching based information exchange

⟺ Information exchange of KP with users

maximum delay, maximum detour, social interests. All this information is published in the M3 space when the driver or passenger joins it. Ridesharing broker KP matches the ontology $O_B$ with M3 space content ($I$) and subscribes for the drivers' and passengers' information in M3 space and implements matching between driver paths and passenger locations and destinations Smirnov et al. (2013). Driver and passenger KPs interactively receive this information from the M3 space and provide drivers and passengers with possible fellow travelers including their profiles, meeting points, meeting time, and full recommendations about the route.

The dynamic ridesharing application ontology is presented in Figure 6. It consists of three upper-level classes: "Vehicle", "Actor", and "Path". Class "Vehicle" describes possible vehicles in the dynamic ridesharing application. Every vehicle is characterized by the passengers and cargo capacity and comfort level. The class "Actor" describes possible users in the application and items to delivery. Class "Path" consists of class "Point" that is a class used for route definition and has the properties shown in Figure 6.

*Figure 6. The ontology of the dynamic ridesharing application*

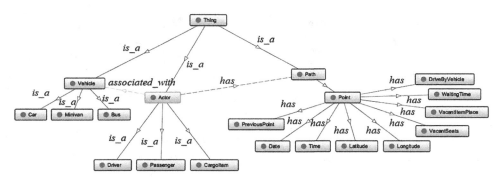

# MOBILE E-TOURISM SERVICES

Internet services in the tourist domain have been becoming more and more popular in recent years. Tourists use such services to book hotels, buy flights, and search for attractions, instead of traditional booking of complete tours through a travel agency. Augmentation of such services with personalized and related situational information is a base for new non-trivial scenarios for use by tourists online and in mobile mode.

Our developed application is a mobile tourist guide acting as a recommendation system, see in details in Smirnov et al. (2014) and Smirnov et al. (2017). Mobile clients are developed for Android devices (smartphones or tablets). The system determines the current tourist location and provides context-aware recommendations about attractions around (e.g., museums, monuments) and their textual and photo description. The user browses attractions and makes decisions on attendance. The personal preferences and the current situation in the region are taken into account. The application also exploits external Internet services for the source of actual information about attractions based on tourists' ratings.

The intelligent mobile tourist guide consists of several M3 KPs, which are united by the smart space technology for providing the tourist with information according to personal preferences (Figure 7). Tourist KP (with the ontology $O_T$) is installed to the user mobile device that shares tourist context with the smart space and provides the tourist results of application operation. Attraction information KP with the ontology $O_{AI}$ that implements retrieving and caching the information about attractions. Recommendation KP with the ontology $O_R$ that evaluates attraction/image/ description scores based on ratings that have been saved to internal database earlier. Region

*Figure 7. The intelligent mobile tourist guide application architecture*

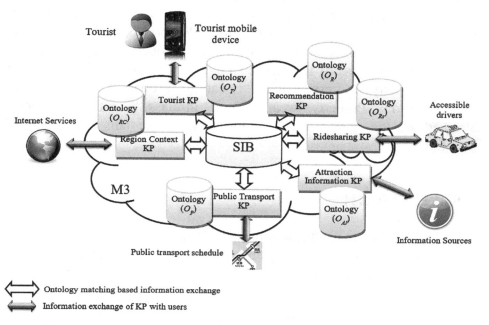

context KP with the ontology $O_{RC}$ that acquires and provides information about current situation in the considered region (e.g., weather, traffic jams, closed attractions). Ridesharing KP with the ontology $O_{Rs}$ that finds matching of the tourist movement with accessible drivers; it provides the tourist possibilities of comfort transportation to the preferred attraction (detailed description of developed algorithm is presented in). Public transport KP with the ontology $O_p$ that finds information about public transport to reach the preferred attraction. Every KP implements the ontology matching procedure of own ontology with the M3 content ($I$) when joins to M3 space that allows to use provided by another services information.

The intelligent mobile tourist guide ontology defines the main concepts and relationships for the application components interaction. It contains classification of attractions (subclasses of the class "Attraction"), different kinds of attraction description (subclasses of class "AttractionDescription"), classification of different transportation means (subclasses of the class "Transportation"), user description (class "User") that can be a tourist (class "Tourist"), location description (class "Location"), and route description (class "Route") that consists of points (class "Point"), which is related to the class "Location". Other relationships between presented classes are depicted in Figure 8. The following main properties have been determined for the ontology. Property "user_id" for the class "User" that specifies identifier for the user in the intelligent mobile tourist guide. Property "role" in class "User" specifies a role that the user has at the moment. Properties "lat" and "long" in class "Location" specify latitude and longitude coordinates of current user location. Property "address" in class "Location". Property "temperature" in class "Location". Property "weather_icon" in class "Location". Property "weather" for the class "Location". Property "traffic_jam_level" in class "Location".

## MOBILE HEALTH

The traditional style of health monitoring and healthcare by visiting a hospital or clinic to meet a doctor is still the most popular. To make healthcare more effective, continuous health monitoring and use personal analysis of the critical

*Figure 8. Ontology of the intelligent mobile tourist guide application*

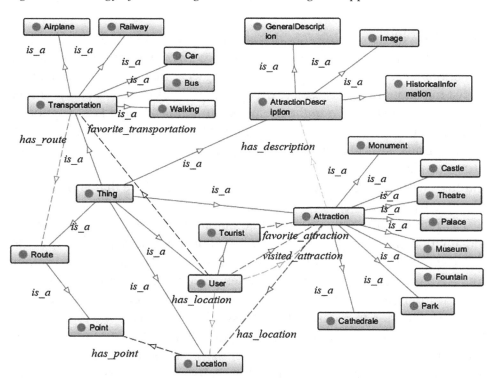

health parameters can be established for the remote patients. This demand drives the development of new approach to healthcare called mobile health. The mobile health application domains is aimed to support and provision of healthcare services using mobile communication devices, such as mobile phones and tablet computers. Mobile devices are primarily responsible for collecting various health parameters data, delivery of healthcare information to medical personnel online. In fact, a mobile health application makes remote users virtually closer to healthcare backend services that have been studied by Borodin et al. (2016), Korzun (2017).

The proposed multi-agent architecture is shown in Figure 9 and described in details by Korzun et al. (2015). Each Patient KP publishes the location of the patient mobile device to the SIB to allow tracking the patient. This KP also makes an alarm either when the user explicitly presses the emergency button, or when dangerous worsening of the heart function is detected by means of automatic processing of the digital electrocardiogram recordings obtained from sensors of the IoT environment. Volunteer KP allows a volunteer to track the movements of the patients under supervision and to receive alarms from Patient KPs. Ambulance KP has similar functions as Volunteer KP, but it has the access to electronic health record information of the patient.

Physician KP enables monitoring of the vital signs of the patient and can be run both on a mobile device and on a stationary computer. Physician obtains the access to the sensor data and implements recordings of electronic health record to M3 space.

There are KPs that provide an interface to external services. Electronic health record KP provides an access to the services of health information systems. Auxiliary Geo-coding Services KP and Map Services KP are intended to identify destinations as the map addresses and construct routes for volunteers and ambulances. The Pharmacy KP is aimed to the obtaining of locations and working hours of nearby pharmacies and, optionally, of lists of available drags and medical equipment.

The last category is the KPs that are neither the agents intended to work with external services, nor the agents intended to provide the information to the end-users. Positioning KP processes the locations of all entities and provides the routes and time estimations. Patient dispatching KP assigns the patients to the volunteers according to proximity metric based on time estimations.

The top-level ontology for the mobile healthcare application is presented in Figure 10. It describes in formal view main entities and determines their interaction in M3 space. The main classes of the ontology are: "Physician", "Ambulance", "Pharmacy", "Patient", "Volunteer", and "Information service".

*Figure 9. The mobile healthcare application architecture*

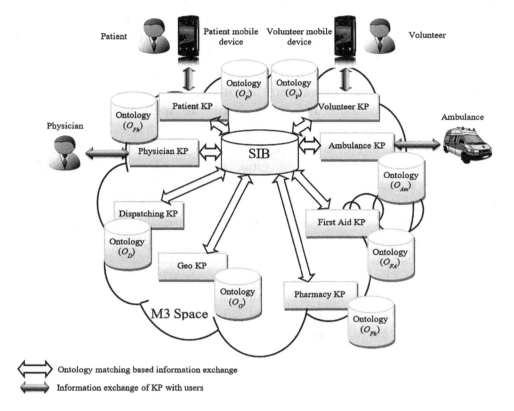

*Figure 10. The ontology of the mobile healthcare application*

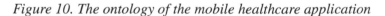

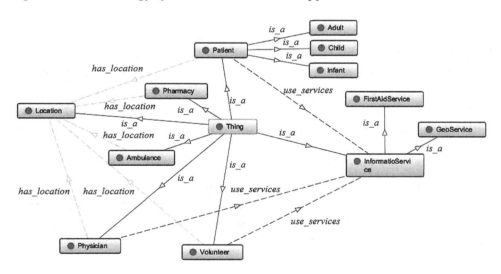

Classes "Physician", "Ambulance", "Pharmacy", "Patient", and "Volunteer" are linked to the class "Location" with relationship "has_location". Classes "Physician", "Patient", and "Volunteer" are linked to the class "Information Services" with relationship "uses_services".

## INDUSTRIAL INTERNET

The fourth industrial revolution (Industry 4.0) - developing a new paradigm of intelligent manufacturing systems based on Internet of Things, internet services, cyber-physical systems, and cloud technologies. For the industrial Internet case study, a two robot interaction scenario for a lens assembly configuration workstation has been chosen. The scenario is described in details by Kashevnik et al. (2015) and Kashevnik et al. (2016) The scenario consists of two robots: pick-and-place and assembly. For both robots, a controlling software has been developed. For their interaction, the M3 space has been used. Let us consider of the workstation "Configuration and assembly gluing "the lens in the frame" (Configuration Workstation). Robot *R1* (Figure 11) receives an order from a warehouse (Figure 11, Warehouse). There are two containers are accessible in warehouse: container with lenses and container with frames. The robot *R1* takes from warehouse a container with frames and puts it to the self-controlled shuttle located at the *S1* (Figure 11, *S1*). When the shuttle leaves *S1* the robot *R1* puts to the next shuttle container with lenses. Both shuttles are going to the Configuration Workstation. In this workstation robot *R2* (Figure 11) transfers containers to the workstation "Packaging arrangement".

The Robot *R3* (Figure 11) performs assembly manufacturing operations at the workstation. After complete assembly, the container is transferred to the Gluing Workstation (Figure 11, Gluing Workstation). Then the glued unit (lens in frame) is installed in the container. The algorithm is repeated for all glues. After this operation, the Robot *R2* (Figure 11) shifts containers on an empty shuttle, located at the workstation. The shuttle is moved to the next workstation.

After completing described operations in *Zone 1* shuttle with details is transferred to *Zone 2*. In *Zone 2* workstations perform other technological operations, up to the final product assembly.

This paper considers the process of *R1* and *R2*'s robot interaction at the configuration workstation where the equipment units "Lenses in the frames" are produced. Components for these units are the "Lens" and "Frame".

*Figure 11. Automated assembly line "3AL"*

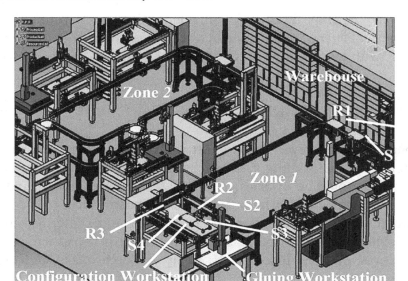

The reference model of cyber-physical system for lenses assembly is presented in Figure 12. The robots are participated in joint scenario for lenses assembly in physical space while they are interacting and coordinating their activities in smart space. Every robot has physical part that implement manipulations in physical space and controller that interacts with the special service through the REST API protocol. Special service represents the robot in the smart space.

Every robot uploads its own ontology to the M3 space when connects to the system. The ontology represents the robot model in smart space. It contains information about robot requirements and possibilities. Requirements represent the information that robot has to get for starting it scenario. Possibilities is the information that robots can provide related to the considered system. The ontology library in smart space merges the different ontologies uploaded by the interacted robots.

Software for robots control consists of a dispatcher module and several executive modules. This software is uploaded to the special controller that implements the robot control. The dispatcher processes control actions and choose related executive module that implements specific technological operations. Control action is determined by marker words and has the following structure: device number, program number, parameter #1 value, parameter #2 value, and parameter #3 value. To implement the action data flag should be

*Figure 12. Reference model of robots interaction in the cyber-physical system*

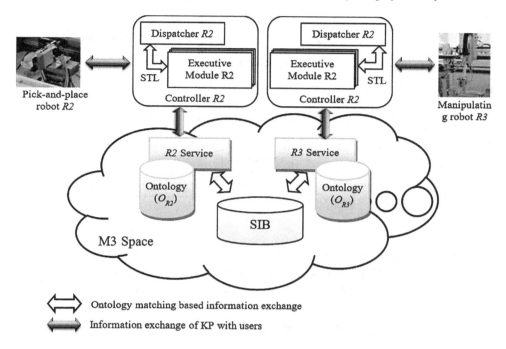

set to "1". Current robot's state can be determined by execution flag value. If it is "1" then command is finished. If it is "0" then command is running.

The ontology for robot interaction in automated assembly line is presented in Figure 13 and reflects main concepts of the modelled process. It includes classes for technological objects: class "Warehouse" for describing the current state and parts stored in warehouse; class "Transport Line" for describing position of shuttles and details loaded in them; class "Case Assembly Workstation", and class "Final Assembly Workstation" for describing the assembly process on each workstation. Ontology also includes classes for details, units and products, that describe their main characteristics and relationships between them (see Figure 13).

## SOLUTIONS AND RECOMMENDATIONS

Application development on top of M3 space are based on the concept of semantic-based information sharing between participants using the publish / subscribe mechanism. M3 spaces are applicable for the small and medium

*Figure 13. Ontology for robot interaction in the cyber-physical system*

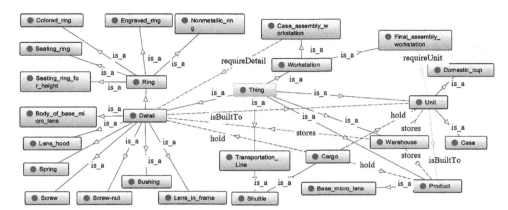

range of IoT applications. In such kind of applications, the participants need to be "smart" and interact with each other for collaboration. For semantic interoperability support the ontologies should be used for participant interaction in M3 space. The provided application case studies can serve as reference models for smart space based application development.

## FUTURE RESEARCH DIRECTIONS

Nowadays, IoT-based applications becomes more and more popular, while the settings of IoT environments leads to complicated challenges that have to be solved both on platform level (e.g., Smart-M3) and application level (KPs that construct services). Development of M3 space applications is based on semantic interoperability platforms provides possibilities of joint tasks solving based collaboration between different participants. For the future research direction, the enhancement of Smart-M3 platform can be considered due to support the participants interaction in a large range IoT-based domain.

An interesting issue that the provided application case studies illustrated is the role of surrounding devices. In addition to "typical" computers (e.g., servers, Internet hosts, local desktops), many other processing units become available, especially in the form of smart IoT objects. The great challenge is how to combine them into a system for service construction and delivery. This issue is closely related to the emerging concept of fog computing and edge-centric computing.

Unified ontology-driven programming methods are required for the needs of many application developers in the emerging Smart Spaces area. The methods should keep the efficiency for practical setting of IoT environments and related challenges of smart spaces deployment in the Internet of Things.

## CONCLUSION

As we have seen throughout this book the spectrum of applications that can be developed using the Smart Spaces concept is very wide. Variants of possible services are only limited by our imagination. The chapter presented six main application domains in the area of IoT applications: collaborative work environments, social networking, transport logistics, mobile e-Tourism services, mobile health, and industrial Internet application domains. These domains were selected based on our more than ten years' experience of using the Smart-M3 platform as an open source solution for smart spaces development. For every application domain, a short description, reference model, and ontology for smart services interaction in an M3 space has been described. Developed application prototypes showed that the M3 space concept is applicable for small and medium range of IoT-based domain.

## REFERENCES

Atzori, L., Iera, A., & Morabito, G. (2010). The Internet of Things: A survey. *Computer Networks*, *54*(15), 2787–2805. doi:10.1016/j.comnet.2010.05.010

Borodin, A., Lebedev, N., Vasilyev, A., Zavyalova, Y., & Korzun, D. (2016). An Experimental Study of Personalized Mobile Assistance Service in Healthcare Emergency Situations. *Proceedings of the Tenth International Conference on Mobile Ubiquitous Computing, Systems, Services and Technologies* (pp. 178-183).

Cook, D., & Das, S. (2007). How smart are our environments? An updated look at the state of the art. *Pervasive and Mobile Computing*, *3*(2), 53–73. doi:10.1016/j.pmcj.2006.12.001

Gilman, E., Davidyuk, O., Su, X., & Riekki, J. (2013). Towards interactive smart spaces. *Journal of Ambient Intelligence and Smart Environments*, *5*(1), 5–22.

Gubbi, J., Buyya, R., Marusic, S., & Palaniswami, M. (2013). Internet of Things (IoT): A vision, architectural elements, and future directions. *Future Generation Computer Systems, 29*(7), 1645–1660. doi:10.1016/j.future.2013.01.010

Kashevnik, A., Teslya, N., Padun, B., Kipriyanov, K., & Arckhipov, V. (2015). Industrial Cyber-Physical System for Lenses Assembly: Configuration Workstation Scenario. *Proceedings of the 17th Conference of the Open Innovations Association FRUCT* (pp. 62–67). doi:10.1109/FRUCT.2015.7117973

Kashevnik, A., Teslya, N., & Shilov, N. (2012). Smart Space Logistic Service for Real-Time Ridesharing. *Proceedings of 11th Conference of Open Innovations Association FRUCT,* St. Petersburg, Russia (pp. 53–62). .

Kashevnik, A., Teslya, N., Yablochnikov, E., Arckhipov, V., & Kipriyanov, K. (2016). Hybrid Automated Line Workstations Interaction Scenario for Optical Devices Assembly. *Proceeding of the 18th Conference of Open Innovations Associations FRUCT,* St. Petersburg, Russia, ITMO University (pp. 92–99). doi:10.1109/FRUCT-ISPIT.2016.7561513

Kortuem, G., Kawsar, F., Sundramoorthy, V., & Fitton, D. (2010). Smart objects as building blocks for the Internet of Things. *IEEE Internet Computing, 14*(1), 44–51. doi:10.1109/MIC.2009.143

Korzun, D. (2017). Internet of Things Meets Mobile Health Systems in Smart Spaces: An Overview. *Internet of Things and Big Data Technologies for Next Generation Healthcare, 23,* 111–129. doi:10.1007/978-3-319-49736-5_6

Korzun, D., Balandin, S., & Gurtov, A. (2013). Deployment of Smart Spaces in Internet of Things: Overview of the Design Challenges. *Internet of Things, Smart Spaces, and Next Generation Networking. Springer, LNCS, 8121,* 48–59.

Korzun, D., Borodin, A., Paramonov, I., Vasilyev, A., & Balandin, S. (2015). Smart Space Enabled Mobile Healthcare Services in Internet of Things Environments. International Journal of Embedded and Real-Time Communication Systems, 6(1).

Korzun, D., Galov, I., & Balandin, S. (2012). Proactive Personalized Mobile Mutli-Blogging Service on SmartM3. *Journal of Computing and Information Technology, 20*(3), 175–182. doi:10.2498/cit.1002094

Manyika, J., Chui, M., Bisson, P., Woetzel, J., Dobbs, R., Bughin, J., Aharon, D. (2015). Unlocking the potential of the Internet of Things. McKinsey Global Institute Report.

Oliver, I., & Boldyrev, S. (2009). Operations on spaces of information. *Proceedings IEEE International Conference on Semantic Computing* (pp. 267–274). IEEE Computer Society.

Smirnov, A., Kashevnik, A., Shilov, N., Paloheimo, H., Waris, H., & Balandin, S. (2010). Smart Space-Driven Sustainable Logistics: Ontology and Major Components. *Proceedings of the 8th Conference of Open Innovations Framework Program FRUCT,* St. Petersburg, Saint-Petersburg State University of Aerospace Instrumentation (pp. 184–194).

Smirnov, A., Kashevnik, A., Shilov, N., & Teslya, N. (2011). Just-in-time Logistics Based on Dynamic Ridesharing Principles. Proceedings Research and Education in Logistics and Supply Chain Management: the Current Situation and New Perspectives, St. Petersburg, Russia (pp. 144-147).

Smirnov, A., Kashevnik, A., Shilov, N., Teslya, N., & Shabaev, A. (2014). Mobile Application for Guiding Tourist Activities: Tourist Assistant – TAIS. *Proceedings of the 16th Conference of Open Innovations Association FRUCT,* St. Petersburg, ITMO University (pp. 94-100).

Smirnov, A., Shilov, N., Kashevnik, A., & Ponomarev, A. (2017). Cyber-physical infomobility for tourism application. *International Journal of Information Technology and Management*, *16*(1), 31–52. doi:10.1504/ IJITM.2017.080949

Smirnov, A., Shilov, N., Kashevnik, A., & Teslya, N. (2012). Smart Logistic Service for Dynamic Ridesharing. In *Internet of Things, Smart Spaces, and Next Generation Networking , LNCS* (Vol. *7469*, pp. 140–151). *Springer.*

Smirnov, A., Shilov, N., Kashevnik, A., Teslya, N., & Laizane, S. (2013). Smart Space-based Ridesharing Service in e-Tourism Application for Karelia Region Accessibility. *Proceedings 8th International Joint Conference on Software Technologies,* Reykjavik, Iceland (pp. 591-598).

Wang, J., Zhu, Q., & Ma, Y. (2013). An agent-based hybrid service delivery for coordinating internet of things and 3rd party service providers. *Journal of Network and Computer Applications*, *36*(6), 1684–1695. doi:10.1016/j. jnca.2013.04.014

# KEY TERMS AND DEFINITIONS

**Collaborative Activity:** Group of people effectively communicates with each other's for working together, to provide own resources to the collective solving process, and access assisting services in the workspace.

**Industrial Internet:** A new paradigm of intelligent manufacturing systems based on Internet of Things, internet services, cyber-physical systems, and cloud technologies.

**Mobile Health:** Modern research and development topic related to joint together information from different body sensors for analyzing it and provide recommendations related to human health.

**Ontology:** Formally represents knowledge as a set of concepts within a domain, using a shared vocabulary to denote the types, properties, and interrelationships of those concepts.

**Smart Space:** An emerging paradigm for application development in the various domains of ubiquitous, pervasive, mobile, embedded, and edge-centric computing.

**Social Networking:** People are communicating in social space using proactive, personalized, and composite services.

# Related Readings

To continue IGI Global's long-standing tradition of advancing innovation through emerging research, please find below a compiled list of recommended IGI Global book chapters and journal articles in the areas of data storage, decentralized computing, and the internet of things. These related readings will provide additional information and guidance to further enrich your knowledge and assist you with your own research.

Abidi, N., Bandyopadhayay, A., & Gupta, V. (2017). Sustainable Supply Chain Management: A Three Dimensional Framework and Performance Metric for Indian IT Product Companies. *International Journal of Information Systems and Supply Chain Management*, *10*(1), 29–52. doi:10.4018/IJISSCM.2017010103

Achahbar, O., & Abid, M. R. (2015). The Impact of Virtualization on High Performance Computing Clustering in the Cloud. *International Journal of Distributed Systems and Technologies*, *6*(4), 65–81. doi:10.4018/IJDST.2015100104

Adhikari, M., Das, A., & Mukherjee, A. (2016). Utility Computing and Its Utilization. In G. Deka, G. Siddesh, K. Srinivasa, & L. Patnaik (Eds.), *Emerging Research Surrounding Power Consumption and Performance Issues in Utility Computing* (pp. 1–21). Hershey, PA: IGI Global. doi:10.4018/978-1-4666-8853-7.ch001

Aggarwal, S., & Nayak, A. (2016). Mobile Big Data: A New Frontier of Innovation. In J. Aguado, C. Feijóo, & I. Martínez (Eds.), *Emerging Perspectives on the Mobile Content Evolution* (pp. 138–158). Hershey, PA: IGI Global. doi:10.4018/978-1-4666-8838-4.ch008

Akherfi, K., Harroud, H., & Gerndt, M. (2016). A Mobile Cloud Middleware to Support Mobility and Cloud Interoperability. *International Journal of Adaptive, Resilient and Autonomic Systems*, *7*(1), 41–58. doi:10.4018/IJARAS.2016010103

Al-Hamami, M. A. (2015). The Impact of Big Data on Security. In A. Al-Hamami & G. Waleed al-Saadoon (Eds.), *Handbook of Research on Threat Detection and Countermeasures in Network Security* (pp. 276–298). Hershey, PA: IGI Global. doi:10.4018/978-1-4666-6583-5.ch015

Al Jabri, H. A., Al-Badi, A. H., & Ali, O. (2017). Exploring the Usage of Big Data Analytical Tools in Telecommunication Industry in Oman. *Information Resources Management Journal*, *30*(1), 1–14. doi:10.4018/IRMJ.2017010101

Alohali, B. (2016). Security in Cloud of Things (CoT). In Z. Ma (Ed.), *Managing Big Data in Cloud Computing Environments* (pp. 46–70). Hershey, PA: IGI Global. doi:10.4018/978-1-4666-9834-5.ch003

Alohali, B. (2017). Detection Protocol of Possible Crime Scenes Using Internet of Things (IoT). In M. Moore (Ed.), *Cybersecurity Breaches and Issues Surrounding Online Threat Protection* (pp. 175–196). Hershey, PA: IGI Global. doi:10.4018/978-1-5225-1941-6.ch008

AlZain, M. A., Li, A. S., Soh, B., & Pardede, E. (2015). Multi-Cloud Data Management using Shamirs Secret Sharing and Quantum Byzantine Agreement Schemes. *International Journal of Cloud Applications and Computing*, *5*(3), 35–52. doi:10.4018/IJCAC.2015070103

Armstrong, S., & Yampolskiy, R. V. (2017). Security Solutions for Intelligent and Complex Systems. In M. Dawson, M. Eltayeb, & M. Omar (Eds.), *Security Solutions for Hyperconnectivity and the Internet of Things* (pp. 37–88). Hershey, PA: IGI Global. doi:10.4018/978-1-5225-0741-3.ch003

Attasena, V., Harbi, N., & Darmont, J. (2015). A Novel Multi-Secret Sharing Approach for Secure Data Warehousing and On-Line Analysis Processing in the Cloud. *International Journal of Data Warehousing and Mining*, *11*(2), 22–43. doi:10.4018/ijdwm.2015040102

Awad, W. S., & Abdullah, H. M. (2014). Improving the Security of Storage Systems: Bahrain Case Study. *International Journal of Mobile Computing and Multimedia Communications*, *6*(3), 75–105. doi:10.4018/IJMCMC.2014070104

Bagui, S., & Nguyen, L. T. (2015). Database Sharding: To Provide Fault Tolerance and Scalability of Big Data on the Cloud. *International Journal of Cloud Applications and Computing*, *5*(2), 36–52. doi:10.4018/IJCAC.2015040103

Barbierato, E., Gribaudo, M., & Iacono, M. (2016). Modeling and Evaluating the Effects of Big Data Storage Resource Allocation in Global Scale Cloud Architectures. *International Journal of Data Warehousing and Mining*, *12*(2), 1–20. doi:10.4018/IJDWM.2016040101

Barbosa, J. L., Barbosa, D. N., Rigo, S. J., Machado de Oliveira, J., & Junior, S. A. (2017). Collaborative Learning on Decentralized Ubiquitous Environments. In L. Tomei (Ed.), *Exploring the New Era of Technology-Infused Education* (pp. 141–157). Hershey, PA: IGI Global. doi:10.4018/978-1-5225-1709-2.ch009

Benmounah, Z., Meshoul, S., & Batouche, M. (2017). Scalable Differential Evolutionary Clustering Algorithm for Big Data Using Map-Reduce Paradigm. *International Journal of Applied Metaheuristic Computing*, *8*(1), 45–60. doi:10.4018/IJAMC.2017010103

Bhadoria, R. S. (2016). Performance of Enterprise Architecture in Utility Computing. In G. Deka, G. Siddesh, K. Srinivasa, & L. Patnaik (Eds.), *Emerging Research Surrounding Power Consumption and Performance Issues in Utility Computing* (pp. 44–68). Hershey, PA: IGI Global. doi:10.4018/978-1-4666-8853-7.ch003

Bhardwaj, A. (2017). Solutions for Securing End User Data over the Cloud Deployed Applications. In M. Moore (Ed.), *Cybersecurity Breaches and Issues Surrounding Online Threat Protection* (pp. 198–218). Hershey, PA: IGI Global. doi:10.4018/978-1-5225-1941-6.ch009

Bibi, S., Katsaros, D., & Bozanis, P. (2015). Cloud Computing Economics. In V. Díaz, J. Lovelle, & B. García-Bustelo (Eds.), *Handbook of Research on Innovations in Systems and Software Engineering* (pp. 125–149). Hershey, PA: IGI Global. doi:10.4018/978-1-4666-6359-6.ch005

Bihl, T. J., Young, W. A. II, & Weckman, G. R. (2016). Defining, Understanding, and Addressing Big Data. *International Journal of Business Analytics*, *3*(2), 1–32. doi:10.4018/IJBAN.2016040101

Bimonte, S., Sautot, L., Journaux, L., & Faivre, B. (2017). Multidimensional Model Design using Data Mining: A Rapid Prototyping Methodology. *International Journal of Data Warehousing and Mining*, *13*(1), 1–35. doi:10.4018/IJDWM.2017010101

Bruno, G. (2017). A Dataflow-Oriented Modeling Approach to Business Processes. *International Journal of Human Capital and Information Technology Professionals*, *8*(1), 51–65. doi:10.4018/IJHCITP.2017010104

Chande, S. V. (2014). Cloud Database Systems: NoSQL, NewSQL, and Hybrid. In P. Raj & G. Deka (Eds.), *Handbook of Research on Cloud Infrastructures for Big Data Analytics* (pp. 216–231). Hershey, PA: IGI Global. doi:10.4018/978-1-4666-5864-6.ch009

Copie, A. Manațe, B., Munteanu, V. I., & Fortiș, T. (2015). An Internet of Things Governance Architecture with Applications in Healthcare. In F. Xhafa, P. Moore, & G. Tadros (Eds.), Advanced Technological Solutions for E-Health and Dementia Patient Monitoring (pp. 322-344). Hershey, PA: IGI Global. doi:10.4018/978-1-4666-7481-3.ch013

Cordeschi, N., Shojafar, M., Amendola, D., & Baccarelli, E. (2015). Energy-Saving QoS Resource Management of Virtualized Networked Data Centers for Big Data Stream Computing. In S. Bagchi (Ed.), *Emerging Research in Cloud Distributed Computing Systems* (pp. 122–155). Hershey, PA: IGI Global. doi:10.4018/978-1-4666-8213-9.ch004

Costan, A. A., Iancu, B., Rasa, P. C., Radu, A., Peculea, A., & Dadarlat, V. T. (2017). Intercloud: Delivering Innovative Cloud Services. In I. Hosu & I. Iancu (Eds.), *Digital Entrepreneurship and Global Innovation* (pp. 59–78). Hershey, PA: IGI Global. doi:10.4018/978-1-5225-0953-0.ch004

Croatti, A., Ricci, A., & Viroli, M. (2017). Towards a Mobile Augmented Reality System for Emergency Management: The Case of SAFE. *International Journal of Distributed Systems and Technologies*, *8*(1), 46–58. doi:10.4018/IJDST.2017010104

David-West, O. (2016). Information and Communications Technology (ICT) and the Supply Chain. In B. Christiansen (Ed.), *Handbook of Research on Global Supply Chain Management* (pp. 495–515). Hershey, PA: IGI Global. doi:10.4018/978-1-4666-9639-6.ch028

Dawson, M. (2017). Exploring Secure Computing for the Internet of Things, Internet of Everything, Web of Things, and Hyperconnectivity. In M. Dawson, M. Eltayeb, & M. Omar (Eds.), *Security Solutions for Hyperconnectivity and the Internet of Things* (pp. 1–12). Hershey, PA: IGI Global. doi:10.4018/978-1-5225-0741-3.ch001

Delgado, J. C. (2015). An Interoperability Framework for Enterprise Applications in Cloud Environments. In N. Rao (Ed.), *Enterprise Management Strategies in the Era of Cloud Computing* (pp. 26–59). Hershey, PA: IGI Global. doi:10.4018/978-1-4666-8339-6.ch002

Dhal, S. K., Verma, H., & Addya, S. K. (2017). Resource and Energy Efficient Virtual Machine Migration in Cloud Data Centers. In A. Turuk, B. Sahoo, & S. Addya (Eds.), *Resource Management and Efficiency in Cloud Computing Environments* (pp. 210–238). Hershey, PA: IGI Global. doi:10.4018/978-1-5225-1721-4.ch009

Duggirala, S. (2014). Big Data Architecture: Storage and Computation. In P. Raj & G. Deka (Eds.), *Handbook of Research on Cloud Infrastructures for Big Data Analytics* (pp. 129–156). Hershey, PA: IGI Global. doi:10.4018/978-1-4666-5864-6.ch006

Easton, J., & Parmar, R. (2017). Navigating Your Way to the Hybrid Cloud. In J. Chen, Y. Zhang, & R. Gottschalk (Eds.), *Handbook of Research on End-to-End Cloud Computing Architecture Design* (pp. 15–38). Hershey, PA: IGI Global. doi:10.4018/978-1-5225-0759-8.ch002

Elkabbany, G. F., & Rasslan, M. (2017). Security Issues in Distributed Computing System Models. In M. Dawson, M. Eltayeb, & M. Omar (Eds.), *Security Solutions for Hyperconnectivity and the Internet of Things* (pp. 211–259). Hershey, PA: IGI Global. doi:10.4018/978-1-5225-0741-3.ch009

Elkhodr, M., Shahrestani, S., & Cheung, H. (2016). Wireless Enabling Technologies for the Internet of Things. In Q. Hassan (Ed.), *Innovative Research and Applications in Next-Generation High Performance Computing* (pp. 368–396). Hershey, PA: IGI Global. doi:10.4018/978-1-5225-0287-6.ch015

Elkhodr, M., Shahrestani, S., & Cheung, H. (2017). Internet of Things Research Challenges. In M. Dawson, M. Eltayeb, & M. Omar (Eds.), *Security Solutions for Hyperconnectivity and the Internet of Things* (pp. 13–36). Hershey, PA: IGI Global. doi:10.4018/978-1-5225-0741-3.ch002

Erturk, E. (2017). Cloud Computing and Cybersecurity Issues Facing Local Enterprises. In M. Moore (Ed.), *Cybersecurity Breaches and Issues Surrounding Online Threat Protection* (pp. 219–247). Hershey, PA: IGI Global. doi:10.4018/978-1-5225-1941-6.ch010

Ferreira da Silva, R., Glatard, T., & Desprez, F. (2015). Self-Management of Operational Issues for Grid Computing: The Case of the Virtual Imaging Platform. In S. Bagchi (Ed.), *Emerging Research in Cloud Distributed Computing Systems* (pp. 187–221). Hershey, PA: IGI Global. doi:10.4018/978-1-4666-8213-9.ch006

Fu, S., He, L., Liao, X., Huang, C., Li, K., & Chang, C. (2015). Analyzing and Boosting the Data Availability in Decentralized Online Social Networks. *International Journal of Web Services Research, 12*(2), 47–72. doi:10.4018/IJWSR.2015040103

Gao, F., & Zhao, Q. (2014). Big Data Based Logistics Data Mining Platform: Architecture and Implementation. *International Journal of Interdisciplinary Telecommunications and Networking, 6*(4), 24–34. doi:10.4018/IJITN.2014100103

Gudivada, V. N., Nandigam, J., & Paris, J. (2015). Programming Paradigms in High Performance Computing. In R. Segall, J. Cook, & Q. Zhang (Eds.), *Research and Applications in Global Supercomputing* (pp. 303–330). Hershey, PA: IGI Global. doi:10.4018/978-1-4666-7461-5.ch013

Hagos, D. H. (2016). Software-Defined Networking for Scalable Cloud-based Services to Improve System Performance of Hadoop-based Big Data Applications. *International Journal of Grid and High Performance Computing, 8*(2), 1–22. doi:10.4018/IJGHPC.2016040101

Hallappanavar, V. L., & Birje, M. N. (2017). Trust Management in Cloud Computing. In M. Dawson, M. Eltayeb, & M. Omar (Eds.), *Security Solutions for Hyperconnectivity and the Internet of Things* (pp. 151–183). Hershey, PA: IGI Global. doi:10.4018/978-1-5225-0741-3.ch007

Hameur Laine, A., & Brahimi, S. (2017). Background on Context-Aware Computing Systems. In C. Reis & M. Maximiano (Eds.), *Internet of Things and Advanced Application in Healthcare* (pp. 1–31). Hershey, PA: IGI Global. doi:10.4018/978-1-5225-1820-4.ch001

Hamidi, H. (2017). A Model for Impact of Organizational Project Benefits Management and its Impact on End User. *Journal of Organizational and End User Computing, 29*(1), 51–65. doi:10.4018/JOEUC.2017010104

Hamidine, H., & Mahmood, A. (2017). Cloud Computing Data Storage Security Based on Different Encryption Schemes. In J. Chen, Y. Zhang, & R. Gottschalk (Eds.), *Handbook of Research on End-to-End Cloud Computing Architecture Design* (pp. 189–221). Hershey, PA: IGI Global. doi:10.4018/978-1-5225-0759-8.ch009

Hamidine, H., & Mahmood, A. (2017). Cloud Computing Data Storage Security Based on Different Encryption Schemes. In J. Chen, Y. Zhang, & R. Gottschalk (Eds.), *Handbook of Research on End-to-End Cloud Computing Architecture Design* (pp. 189–221). Hershey, PA: IGI Global. doi:10.4018/978-1-5225-0759-8.ch009

Hao, Y., & Helo, P. (2015). Cloud Manufacturing towards Sustainable Management. In F. Soliman (Ed.), *Business Transformation and Sustainability through Cloud System Implementation* (pp. 121–139). Hershey, PA: IGI Global. doi:10.4018/978-1-4666-6445-6.ch009

Hasan, N., & Rahman, A. A. (2017). Ranking the Factors that Impact Customers Online Participation in Value Co-creation in Service Sector Using Analytic Hierarchy Process. *International Journal of Information Systems in the Service Sector, 9*(1), 37–53. doi:10.4018/IJISSS.2017010103

Hashemi, S., Monfaredi, K., & Hashemi, S. Y. (2015). Cloud Computing for Secure Services in E-Government Architecture. *Journal of Information Technology Research, 8*(1), 43–61. doi:10.4018/JITR.2015010104

Hayajneh, S. M. (2015). Cloud Computing SaaS Paradigm for Efficient Modelling of Solar Features and Activities. *International Journal of Cloud Applications and Computing, 5*(3), 20–34. doi:10.4018/IJCAC.2015070102

Huang, L. K. (2017). A Cultural Model of Online Banking Adoption: Long-Term Orientation Perspective. *Journal of Organizational and End User Computing, 29*(1), 1–22. doi:10.4018/JOEUC.2017010101

Jacob, G., & Annamalai, M. (2017). Secure Storage and Transmission of Healthcare Records. In V. Tiwari, B. Tiwari, R. Thakur, & S. Gupta (Eds.), *Pattern and Data Analysis in Healthcare Settings* (pp. 7–34). Hershey, PA: IGI Global. doi:10.4018/978-1-5225-0536-5.ch002

Jadon, K. S., Mudgal, P., & Bhadoria, R. S. (2016). Optimization and Management of Resource in Utility Computing. In G. Deka, G. Siddesh, K. Srinivasa, & L. Patnaik (Eds.), *Emerging Research Surrounding Power Consumption and Performance Issues in Utility Computing* (pp. 22–43). Hershey, PA: IGI Global. doi:10.4018/978-1-4666-8853-7.ch002

Jararweh, Y., Al-Sharqawi, O., Abdulla, N., Tawalbeh, L., & Alhammouri, M. (2014). High-Throughput Encryption for Cloud Computing Storage System. *International Journal of Cloud Applications and Computing*, *4*(2), 1–14. doi:10.4018/ijcac.2014040101

Jha, M., Jha, S., & O'Brien, L. (2017). Social Media and Big Data: A Conceptual Foundation for Organizations. In R. Chugh (Ed.), *Harnessing Social Media as a Knowledge Management Tool* (pp. 315–332). Hershey, PA: IGI Global. doi:10.4018/978-1-5225-0495-5.ch015

Kantarci, B., & Mouftah, H. T. (2015). Sensing as a Service in Cloud-Centric Internet of Things Architecture. In T. Soyata (Ed.), *Enabling Real-Time Mobile Cloud Computing through Emerging Technologies* (pp. 83–115). Hershey, PA: IGI Global. doi:10.4018/978-1-4666-8662-5.ch003

Kasemsap, K. (2015). The Role of Cloud Computing Adoption in Global Business. In V. Chang, R. Walters, & G. Wills (Eds.), *Delivery and Adoption of Cloud Computing Services in Contemporary Organizations* (pp. 26–55). Hershey, PA: IGI Global. doi:10.4018/978-1-4666-8210-8.ch002

Kasemsap, K. (2015). The Role of Cloud Computing in Global Supply Chain. In N. Rao (Ed.), *Enterprise Management Strategies in the Era of Cloud Computing* (pp. 192–219). Hershey, PA: IGI Global. doi:10.4018/978-1-4666-8339-6.ch009

Kasemsap, K. (2017). Mastering Intelligent Decision Support Systems in Enterprise Information Management. In G. Sreedhar (Ed.), *Web Data Mining and the Development of Knowledge-Based Decision Support Systems* (pp. 35–56). Hershey, PA: IGI Global. doi:10.4018/978-1-5225-1877-8.ch004

Kaukalias, T., & Chatzimisios, P. (2015). Internet of Things (IoT). In M. Khosrow-Pour (Ed.), *Encyclopedia of Information Science and Technology* (3rd ed., pp. 7623–7632). Hershey, PA: IGI Global. doi:10.4018/978-1-4666-5888-2.ch751

Kavoura, A., & Koziol, L. (2017). Polish Firms' Innovation Capability for Competitiveness via Information Technologies and Social Media Implementation. In A. Vlachvei, O. Notta, K. Karantininis, & N. Tsounis (Eds.), *Factors Affecting Firm Competitiveness and Performance in the Modern Business World* (pp. 191–222). Hershey, PA: IGI Global. doi:10.4018/978-1-5225-0843-4.ch007

Khan, I. U., Hameed, Z., & Khan, S. U. (2017). Understanding Online Banking Adoption in a Developing Country: UTAUT2 with Cultural Moderators. *Journal of Global Information Management*, 25(1), 43–65. doi:10.4018/JGIM.2017010103

Kirci, P. (2017). Ubiquitous and Cloud Computing: Ubiquitous Computing. In A. Turuk, B. Sahoo, & S. Addya (Eds.), *Resource Management and Efficiency in Cloud Computing Environments* (pp. 1–32). Hershey, PA: IGI Global. doi:10.4018/978-1-5225-1721-4.ch001

Kofahi, I., & Alryalat, H. (2017). Enterprise Resource Planning (ERP) Implementation Approaches and the Performance of Procure-to-Pay Business Processes: (Field Study in Companies that Implement Oracle ERP in Jordan). *International Journal of Information Technology Project Management*, 8(1), 55–71. doi:10.4018/IJITPM.2017010104

Koumaras, H., Damaskos, C., Diakoumakos, G., Kourtis, M., Xilouris, G., Gardikis, G., & Siakoulis, T. et al. (2015). Virtualization Evolution: From IT Infrastructure Abstraction of Cloud Computing to Virtualization of Network Functions. In G. Mastorakis, C. Mavromoustakis, & E. Pallis (Eds.), *Resource Management of Mobile Cloud Computing Networks and Environments* (pp. 279–306). Hershey, PA: IGI Global. doi:10.4018/978-1-4666-8225-2.ch010

Kuada, E. (2017). Security and Trust in Cloud Computing. In M. Dawson, M. Eltayeb, & M. Omar (Eds.), *Security Solutions for Hyperconnectivity and the Internet of Things* (pp. 184–210). Hershey, PA: IGI Global. doi:10.4018/978-1-5225-0741-3.ch008

Kumar, D., Sahoo, B., & Mandal, T. (2015). Heuristic Task Consolidation Techniques for Energy Efficient Cloud Computing. In N. Rao (Ed.), *Enterprise Management Strategies in the Era of Cloud Computing* (pp. 238–260). Hershey, PA: IGI Global. doi:10.4018/978-1-4666-8339-6.ch011

Lee, C. K., Cao, Y., & Ng, K. H. (2017). Big Data Analytics for Predictive Maintenance Strategies. In H. Chan, N. Subramanian, & M. Abdulrahman (Eds.), *Supply Chain Management in the Big Data Era* (pp. 50–74). Hershey, PA: IGI Global. doi:10.4018/978-1-5225-0956-1.ch004

Liao, W. (2016). Application of Hadoop in the Document Storage Management System for Telecommunication Enterprise. *International Journal of Interdisciplinary Telecommunications and Networking*, 8(2), 58–68. doi:10.4018/IJITN.2016040106

Liew, C. S., Ang, J. M., Goh, Y. T., Koh, W. K., Tan, S. Y., & Teh, R. Y. (2017). Factors Influencing Consumer Acceptance of Internet of Things Technology. In N. Suki (Ed.), *Handbook of Research on Leveraging Consumer Psychology for Effective Customer Engagement* (pp. 186–201). Hershey, PA: IGI Global. doi:10.4018/978-1-5225-0746-8.ch012

Lytras, M. D., Raghavan, V., & Damiani, E. (2017). Big Data and Data Analytics Research: From Metaphors to Value Space for Collective Wisdom in Human Decision Making and Smart Machines. *International Journal on Semantic Web and Information Systems*, 13(1), 1–10. doi:10.4018/IJSWIS.2017010101

Mabe, L. K., & Oladele, O. I. (2017). Application of Information Communication Technologies for Agricultural Development through Extension Services: A Review. In T. Tossy (Ed.), *Information Technology Integration for Socio-Economic Development* (pp. 52–101). Hershey, PA: IGI Global. doi:10.4018/978-1-5225-0539-6.ch003

Machaka, P., & Nelwamondo, F. (2016). Data Mining Techniques for Distributed Denial of Service Attacks Detection in the Internet of Things: A Research Survey. In O. Isafiade & A. Bagula (Eds.), *Data Mining Trends and Applications in Criminal Science and Investigations* (pp. 275–334). Hershey, PA: IGI Global. doi:10.4018/978-1-5225-0463-4.ch010

Manohari, P. K., & Ray, N. K. (2017). A Comprehensive Study of Security in Cloud Computing. In N. Ray & A. Turuk (Eds.), *Handbook of Research on Advanced Wireless Sensor Network Applications, Protocols, and Architectures* (pp. 386–412). Hershey, PA: IGI Global. doi:10.4018/978-1-5225-0486-3.ch016

Manvi, S. S., & Hegde, N. (2017). Vehicular Cloud Computing Challenges and Security. In S. Bhattacharyya, N. Das, D. Bhattacharjee, & A. Mukherjee (Eds.), *Handbook of Research on Recent Developments in Intelligent Communication Application* (pp. 344–365). Hershey, PA: IGI Global. doi:10.4018/978-1-5225-1785-6.ch013

McKelvey, N., Curran, K., & Subaginy, N. (2015). The Internet of Things. In M. Khosrow-Pour (Ed.), *Encyclopedia of Information Science and Technology* (3rd ed., pp. 5777–5783). Hershey, PA: IGI Global. doi:10.4018/978-1-4666-5888-2.ch570

Meddah, I. H., Belkadi, K., & Boudia, M. A. (2017). Efficient Implementation of Hadoop MapReduce based Business Process Dataflow. *International Journal of Decision Support System Technology*, *9*(1), 49–60. doi:10.4018/IJDSST.2017010104

Meghanathan, N. (2015). Virtualization as the Catalyst for Cloud Computing. In M. Khosrow-Pour (Ed.), *Encyclopedia of Information Science and Technology* (3rd ed., pp. 1096–1110). Hershey, PA: IGI Global. doi:10.4018/978-1-4666-5888-2.ch105

Mehenni, T. (2017). Geographic Knowledge Discovery in Multiple Spatial Databases. In S. Faiz & K. Mahmoudi (Eds.), *Handbook of Research on Geographic Information Systems Applications and Advancements* (pp. 344–366). Hershey, PA: IGI Global. doi:10.4018/978-1-5225-0937-0.ch013

Mehrotra, S., & Kohli, S. (2017). Data Clustering and Various Clustering Approaches. In S. Bhattacharyya, S. De, I. Pan, & P. Dutta (Eds.), *Intelligent Multidimensional Data Clustering and Analysis* (pp. 90–108). Hershey, PA: IGI Global. doi:10.4018/978-1-5225-1776-4.ch004

Meralto, C., Moura, J., & Marinheiro, R. (2017). Wireless Mesh Sensor Networks with Mobile Devices: A Comprehensive Review. In N. Ray & A. Turuk (Eds.), *Handbook of Research on Advanced Wireless Sensor Network Applications, Protocols, and Architectures* (pp. 129–155). Hershey, PA: IGI Global. doi:10.4018/978-1-5225-0486-3.ch005

Moradbeikie, A., Abrishami, S., & Abbasi, H. (2016). Creating Time-Limited Attributes for Time-Limited Services in Cloud Computing. *International Journal of Information Security and Privacy*, *10*(4), 44–57. doi:10.4018/IJISP.2016100103

Mourtzoukos, K., Kefalakis, N., & Soldatos, J. (2015). Open Source Object Directory Services for Inter-Enterprise Tracking and Tracing Applications. In I. Lee (Ed.), *RFID Technology Integration for Business Performance Improvement* (pp. 80–97). Hershey, PA: IGI Global. doi:10.4018/978-1-4666-6308-4.ch004

Mugisha, E., Zhang, G., El Abidine, M. Z., & Eugene, M. (2017). A TPM-based Secure Multi-Cloud Storage Architecture grounded on Erasure Codes. *International Journal of Information Security and Privacy, 11*(1), 52–64. doi:10.4018/IJISP.2017010104

Munir, K. (2017). Security Model for Mobile Cloud Database as a Service (DBaaS). In K. Munir (Ed.), *Security Management in Mobile Cloud Computing* (pp. 169–180). Hershey, PA: IGI Global. doi:10.4018/978-1-5225-0602-7.ch008

Murugaiyan, S. R., Chandramohan, D., Vengattaraman, T., & Dhavachelvan, P. (2014). A Generic Privacy Breach Preventing Methodology for Cloud Based Web Service. *International Journal of Grid and High Performance Computing, 6*(3), 53–84. doi:10.4018/ijghpc.2014070104

Naeem, M. A., & Jamil, N. (2015). Online Processing of End-User Data in Real-Time Data Warehousing. In M. Usman (Ed.), *Improving Knowledge Discovery through the Integration of Data Mining Techniques* (pp. 13–31). Hershey, PA: IGI Global. doi:10.4018/978-1-4666-8513-0.ch002

Nayak, P. (2017). Internet of Things Services, Applications, Issues, and Challenges. In N. Ray & A. Turuk (Eds.), *Handbook of Research on Advanced Wireless Sensor Network Applications, Protocols, and Architectures* (pp. 353–368). Hershey, PA: IGI Global. doi:10.4018/978-1-5225-0486-3.ch014

Nekaj, E. L. (2017). The Crowd Economy: From the Crowd to Businesses to Public Administrations and Multinational Companies. In W. Vassallo (Ed.), *Crowdfunding for Sustainable Entrepreneurship and Innovation* (pp. 1–19). Hershey, PA: IGI Global. doi:10.4018/978-1-5225-0568-6.ch001

Omar, M. (2015). Cloud Computing Security: Abuse and Nefarious Use of Cloud Computing. In K. Munir, M. Al-Mutairi, & L. Mohammed (Eds.), *Handbook of Research on Security Considerations in Cloud Computing* (pp. 30–38). Hershey, PA: IGI Global. doi:10.4018/978-1-4666-8387-7.ch002

Orike, S., & Brown, D. (2016). Big Data Management: An Investigation into Wireless and Cloud Computing. *International Journal of Interdisciplinary Telecommunications and Networking*, 8(4), 34–50. doi:10.4018/IJITN.2016100104

Ouf, S., & Nasr, M. (2015). Cloud Computing: The Future of Big Data Management. *International Journal of Cloud Applications and Computing*, 5(2), 53–61. doi:10.4018/IJCAC.2015040104

Ozpinar, A., & Yarkan, S. (2016). Vehicle to Cloud: Big Data for Environmental Sustainability, Energy, and Traffic Management. In M. Singh, & D. G. (Eds.), *Effective Big Data Management and Opportunities for Implementation* (pp. 182-201). Hershey, PA: IGI Global. doi:10.4018/978-1-5225-0182-4.ch012

Pal, A., & Kumar, M. (2017). Collaborative Filtering Based Data Mining for Large Data. In V. Bhatnagar (Ed.), *Collaborative Filtering Using Data Mining and Analysis* (pp. 115–127). Hershey, PA: IGI Global. doi:10.4018/978-1-5225-0489-4.ch006

Pal, K., & Karakostas, B. (2016). A Game-Based Approach for Simulation and Design of Supply Chains. In T. Kramberger, V. Potočan, & V. Ipavec (Eds.), *Sustainable Logistics and Strategic Transportation Planning* (pp. 1–23). Hershey, PA: IGI Global. doi:10.4018/978-1-5225-0001-8.ch001

Panda, S. (2017). Security Issues and Challenges in Internet of Things. In N. Ray & A. Turuk (Eds.), *Handbook of Research on Advanced Wireless Sensor Network Applications, Protocols, and Architectures* (pp. 369–385). Hershey, PA: IGI Global. doi:10.4018/978-1-5225-0486-3.ch015

Pandit, S., Milman, I., Oberhofer, M., & Zhou, Y. (2017). Principled Reference Data Management for Big Data and Business Intelligence. *International Journal of Organizational and Collective Intelligence*, 7(1), 47–66. doi:10.4018/IJOCI.2017010104

Paul, A. K., & Sahoo, B. (2017). Dynamic Virtual Machine Placement in Cloud Computing. In A. Turuk, B. Sahoo, & S. Addya (Eds.), *Resource Management and Efficiency in Cloud Computing Environments* (pp. 136–167). Hershey, PA: IGI Global. doi:10.4018/978-1-5225-1721-4.ch006

Petri, I., Diaz-Montes, J., Zou, M., Zamani, A. R., Beach, T. H., Rana, O. F., & Rezgui, Y. et al. (2016). Distributed Multi-Cloud Based Building Data Analytics. In G. Kecskemeti, A. Kertesz, & Z. Nemeth (Eds.), *Developing Interoperable and Federated Cloud Architecture* (pp. 143–169). Hershey, PA: IGI Global. doi:10.4018/978-1-5225-0153-4.ch006

Poleto, T., Heuer de Carvalho, V. D., & Costa, A. P. (2017). The Full Knowledge of Big Data in the Integration of Inter-Organizational Information: An Approach Focused on Decision Making. *International Journal of Decision Support System Technology*, 9(1), 16–31. doi:10.4018/IJDSST.2017010102

Rahman, N., & Iverson, S. (2015). Big Data Business Intelligence in Bank Risk Analysis. *International Journal of Business Intelligence Research*, 6(2), 55–77. doi:10.4018/IJBIR.2015070104

Raj, P. (2014). Big Data Analytics Demystified. In P. Raj & G. Deka (Eds.), *Handbook of Research on Cloud Infrastructures for Big Data Analytics* (pp. 38–73). Hershey, PA: IGI Global. doi:10.4018/978-1-4666-5864-6.ch003

Raj, P. (2014). The Compute Infrastructures for Big Data Analytics. In P. Raj & G. Deka (Eds.), *Handbook of Research on Cloud Infrastructures for Big Data Analytics* (pp. 74–109). Hershey, PA: IGI Global. doi:10.4018/978-1-4666-5864-6.ch004

Raj, P. (2014). The Network Infrastructures for Big Data Analytics. In P. Raj & G. Deka (Eds.), *Handbook of Research on Cloud Infrastructures for Big Data Analytics* (pp. 157–185). Hershey, PA: IGI Global. doi:10.4018/978-1-4666-5864-6.ch007

Raman, A. C. (2014). Storage Infrastructure for Big Data and Cloud. In P. Raj & G. Deka (Eds.), *Handbook of Research on Cloud Infrastructures for Big Data Analytics* (pp. 110–128). Hershey, PA: IGI Global. doi:10.4018/978-1-4666-5864-6.ch005

Rao, A. P. (2017). Discovering Knowledge Hidden in Big Data from Machine-Learning Techniques. In G. Sreedhar (Ed.), *Web Data Mining and the Development of Knowledge-Based Decision Support Systems* (pp. 167–183). Hershey, PA: IGI Global. doi:10.4018/978-1-5225-1877-8.ch010

Rathore, M. M., Paul, A., Ahmad, A., & Jeon, G. (2017). IoT-Based Big Data: From Smart City towards Next Generation Super City Planning. *International Journal on Semantic Web and Information Systems*, 13(1), 28–47. doi:10.4018/IJSWIS.2017010103

Ratten, V. (2015). An Entrepreneurial Approach to Cloud Computing Design and Application: Technological Innovation and Information System Usage. In S. Aljawarneh (Ed.), *Advanced Research on Cloud Computing Design and Applications* (pp. 1–14). Hershey, PA: IGI Global. doi:10.4018/978-1-4666-8676-2.ch001

Rebekah, R. D., Cheelu, D., & Babu, M. R. (2017). Necessity of Key Aggregation Cryptosystem for Data Sharing in Cloud Computing. In P. Krishna (Ed.), *Emerging Technologies and Applications for Cloud-Based Gaming* (pp. 210–227). Hershey, PA: IGI Global. doi:10.4018/978-1-5225-0546-4.ch010

Rehman, A., Ullah, R., & Abdullah, F. (2015). Big Data Analysis in IoT. In N. Zaman, M. Seliaman, M. Hassan, & F. Marquez (Eds.), *Handbook of Research on Trends and Future Directions in Big Data and Web Intelligence* (pp. 313–327). Hershey, PA: IGI Global. doi:10.4018/978-1-4666-8505-5.ch015

Rehman, M. H., Khan, A. U., & Batool, A. (2016). Big Data Analytics in Mobile and Cloud Computing Environments. In Q. Hassan (Ed.), *Innovative Research and Applications in Next-Generation High Performance Computing* (pp. 349–367). Hershey, PA: IGI Global. doi:10.4018/978-1-5225-0287-6.ch014

Rosado da Cruz, A. M., & Paiva, S. (2016). Cloud and Mobile: A Future Together. In A. Rosado da Cruz & S. Paiva (Eds.), *Modern Software Engineering Methodologies for Mobile and Cloud Environments* (pp. 1–20). Hershey, PA: IGI Global. doi:10.4018/978-1-4666-9916-8.ch001

Rusko, R. (2017). Strategic Turning Points in ICT Business: The Business Development, Transformation, and Evolution in the Case of Nokia. In I. Oncioiu (Ed.), *Driving Innovation and Business Success in the Digital Economy* (pp. 1–15). Hershey, PA: IGI Global. doi:10.4018/978-1-5225-1779-5.ch001

Sahlin, J. P. (2015). Federal Government Application of the Cloud Computing Application Integration Model. In M. Khosrow-Pour (Ed.), *Encyclopedia of Information Science and Technology* (3rd ed., pp. 2735–2744). Hershey, PA: IGI Global. doi:10.4018/978-1-4666-5888-2.ch267

Sahoo, S., Sahoo, B., Turuk, A. K., & Mishra, S. K. (2017). Real Time Task Execution in Cloud Using MapReduce Framework. In A. Turuk, B. Sahoo, & S. Addya (Eds.), *Resource Management and Efficiency in Cloud Computing Environments* (pp. 190–209). Hershey, PA: IGI Global. doi:10.4018/978-1-5225-1721-4.ch008

Schnjakin, M., & Meinel, C. (2014). Solving Security and Availability Challenges in Public Clouds. In A. Kayem & C. Meinel (Eds.), *Information Security in Diverse Computing Environments* (pp. 280–302). Hershey, PA: IGI Global. doi:10.4018/978-1-4666-6158-5.ch015

Shaikh, F. (2017). The Benefits of New Online (Digital) Technologies on Business: Understanding the Impact of Digital on Different Aspects of the Business. In I. Hosu & I. Iancu (Eds.), *Digital Entrepreneurship and Global Innovation* (pp. 1–17). Hershey, PA: IGI Global. doi:10.4018/978-1-5225-0953-0.ch001

Shalan, M. (2017). Cloud Service Footprint (CSF): Utilizing Risk and Governance Directions to Characterize a Cloud Service. In A. Turuk, B. Sahoo, & S. Addya (Eds.), *Resource Management and Efficiency in Cloud Computing Environments* (pp. 61–88). Hershey, PA: IGI Global. doi:10.4018/978-1-5225-1721-4.ch003

Sharma, A., & Tandekar, P. (2017). Cyber Security and Business Growth. In Rajagopal, & R. Behl (Eds.), Business Analytics and Cyber Security Management in Organizations (pp. 14-27). Hershey, PA: IGI Global. doi:10.4018/978-1-5225-0902-8.ch002

Shen, Y., Li, Y., Wu, L., Liu, S., & Wen, Q. (2014). Big Data Techniques, Tools, and Applications. In Y. Shen, Y. Li, L. Wu, S. Liu, & Q. Wen (Eds.), *Enabling the New Era of Cloud Computing: Data Security, Transfer, and Management* (pp. 185–212). Hershey, PA: IGI Global. doi:10.4018/978-1-4666-4801-2.ch009

Shen, Y., Li, Y., Wu, L., Liu, S., & Wen, Q. (2014). Cloud Infrastructure: Virtualization. In Y. Shen, Y. Li, L. Wu, S. Liu, & Q. Wen (Eds.), *Enabling the New Era of Cloud Computing: Data Security, Transfer, and Management* (pp. 51–76). Hershey, PA: IGI Global. doi:10.4018/978-1-4666-4801-2.ch003

Siddesh, G. M., Srinivasa, K. G., & Tejaswini, L. (2015). Recent Trends in Cloud Computing Security Issues and Their Mitigation. In G. Deka & S. Bakshi (Eds.), *Handbook of Research on Securing Cloud-Based Databases with Biometric Applications* (pp. 16–46). Hershey, PA: IGI Global. doi:10.4018/978-1-4666-6559-0.ch002

Singh, B., & K.S., J. (2017). Security Management in Mobile Cloud Computing: Security and Privacy Issues and Solutions in Mobile Cloud Computing. In K. Munir (Ed.), *Security Management in Mobile Cloud Computing* (pp. 148-168). Hershey, PA: IGI Global. doi:10.4018/978-1-5225-0602-7.ch007

Singh, J., Gimekar, A. M., & Venkatesan, S. (2017). An Overview of Big Data Security with Hadoop Framework. In M. Kumar (Ed.), *Applied Big Data Analytics in Operations Management* (pp. 165–181). Hershey, PA: IGI Global. doi:10.4018/978-1-5225-0886-1.ch008

Singh, S., & Singh, J. (2017). Management of SME's Semi Structured Data Using Semantic Technique. In M. Kumar (Ed.), *Applied Big Data Analytics in Operations Management* (pp. 133–164). Hershey, PA: IGI Global. doi:10.4018/978-1-5225-0886-1.ch007

Sokolowski, L., & Oussena, S. (2016). Using Big Data in Collaborative Learning. In M. Atzmueller, S. Oussena, & T. Roth-Berghofer (Eds.), *Enterprise Big Data Engineering, Analytics, and Management* (pp. 221–237). Hershey, PA: IGI Global. doi:10.4018/978-1-5225-0293-7.ch013

Soliman, F. (2015). Evaluation of Cloud System Success Factors in Supply-Demand Chains. In F. Soliman (Ed.), *Business Transformation and Sustainability through Cloud System Implementation* (pp. 90–104). Hershey, PA: IGI Global. doi:10.4018/978-1-4666-6445-6.ch007

Srinivasan, S. (2014). Meeting Compliance Requirements while using Cloud Services. In S. Srinivasan (Ed.), *Security, Trust, and Regulatory Aspects of Cloud Computing in Business Environments* (pp. 127–144). Hershey, PA: IGI Global. doi:10.4018/978-1-4666-5788-5.ch007

Sun, X., & Wei, Z. (2015). The Dynamic Data Privacy Protection Strategy Based on the CAP Theory. *International Journal of Interdisciplinary Telecommunications and Networking*, 7(1), 44–56. doi:10.4018/ijitn.2015010104

Sundararajan, S., Bhasi, M., & Pramod, K. (2017). Managing Software Risks in Maintenance Projects, from a Vendor Perspective: A Case Study in Global Software Development. *International Journal of Information Technology Project Management*, 8(1), 35–54. doi:10.4018/IJITPM.2017010103

Sundaresan, M., & Boopathy, D. (2014). Different Perspectives of Cloud Security. In S. Srinivasan (Ed.), *Security, Trust, and Regulatory Aspects of Cloud Computing in Business Environments* (pp. 73–90). Hershey, PA: IGI Global. doi:10.4018/978-1-4666-5788-5.ch004

Sutagundar, A. V., & Hatti, D. (2017). Data Management in Internet of Things. In N. Kamila (Ed.), *Handbook of Research on Wireless Sensor Network Trends, Technologies, and Applications* (pp. 80–97). Hershey, PA: IGI Global. doi:10.4018/978-1-5225-0501-3.ch004

Swacha, J. (2014). Measuring and Managing the Economics of Information Storage. In T. Tsiakis, T. Kargidis, & P. Katsaros (Eds.), *Approaches and Processes for Managing the Economics of Information Systems* (pp. 47–65). Hershey, PA: IGI Global. doi:10.4018/978-1-4666-4983-5.ch003

Swarnkar, M., & Bhadoria, R. S. (2016). Security Aspects in Utility Computing. In G. Deka, G. Siddesh, K. Srinivasa, & L. Patnaik (Eds.), *Emerging Research Surrounding Power Consumption and Performance Issues in Utility Computing* (pp. 262–275). Hershey, PA: IGI Global. doi:10.4018/978-1-4666-8853-7. ch012

Talamantes-Padilla, C. A., García-Alcaráz, J. L., Maldonado-Macías, A. A., Alor-Hernández, G., Sánchéz-Ramírez, C., & Hernández-Arellano, J. L. (2017). Information and Communication Technology Impact on Supply Chain Integration, Flexibility, and Performance. In M. Tavana, K. Szabat, & K. Puranam (Eds.), *Organizational Productivity and Performance Measurements Using Predictive Modeling and Analytics* (pp. 213–234). Hershey, PA: IGI Global. doi:10.4018/978-1-5225-0654-6.ch011

Tang, Z., & Pan, Y. (2015). Big Data Security Management. In N. Zaman, M. Seliaman, M. Hassan, & F. Marquez (Eds.), *Handbook of Research on Trends and Future Directions in Big Data and Web Intelligence* (pp. 53–66). Hershey, PA: IGI Global. doi:10.4018/978-1-4666-8505-5.ch003

Thakur, P. K., & Verma, A. (2015). Process Batch Offloading Method for Mobile-Cloud Computing Platform. *Journal of Cases on Information Technology*, *17*(3), 1–13. doi:10.4018/JCIT.2015070101

Thota, C., Manogaran, G., Lopez, D., & Vijayakumar, V. (2017). Big Data Security Framework for Distributed Cloud Data Centers. In M. Moore (Ed.), *Cybersecurity Breaches and Issues Surrounding Online Threat Protection* (pp. 288–310). Hershey, PA: IGI Global. doi:10.4018/978-1-5225-1941-6.ch012

Toor, G. S., & Ma, M. (2017). Security Issues of Communication Networks in Smart Grid. In M. Ferrag & A. Ahmim (Eds.), *Security Solutions and Applied Cryptography in Smart Grid Communications* (pp. 29–49). Hershey, PA: IGI Global. doi:10.4018/978-1-5225-1829-7.ch002

Wahi, A. K., Medury, Y., & Misra, R. K. (2015). Big Data: Enabler or Challenge for Enterprise 2.0. *International Journal of Service Science, Management, Engineering, and Technology*, *6*(2), 1–17. doi:10.4018/ijssmet.2015040101

Wang, H., Liu, W., & Soyata, T. (2014). Accessing Big Data in the Cloud Using Mobile Devices. In P. Raj & G. Deka (Eds.), *Handbook of Research on Cloud Infrastructures for Big Data Analytics* (pp. 444–470). Hershey, PA: IGI Global. doi:10.4018/978-1-4666-5864-6.ch018

Wang, M., & Kerr, D. (2017). Confidential Data Storage Systems for Wearable Platforms. In A. Marrington, D. Kerr, & J. Gammack (Eds.), *Managing Security Issues and the Hidden Dangers of Wearable Technologies* (pp. 74–97). Hershey, PA: IGI Global. doi:10.4018/978-1-5225-1016-1.ch004

Winter, J. S. (2015). Privacy Challenges for the Internet of Things. In M. Khosrow-Pour (Ed.), *Encyclopedia of Information Science and Technology* (3rd ed., pp. 4373–4383). Hershey, PA: IGI Global. doi:10.4018/978-1-4666-5888-2.ch429

Wolfe, M. (2017). Establishing Governance for Hybrid Cloud and the Internet of Things. In J. Chen, Y. Zhang, & R. Gottschalk (Eds.), *Handbook of Research on End-to-End Cloud Computing Architecture Design* (pp. 300–325). Hershey, PA: IGI Global. doi:10.4018/978-1-5225-0759-8.ch013

Yan, Z. (2014). Trust Management in Mobile Cloud Computing. In *Trust Management in Mobile Environments: Autonomic and Usable Models* (pp. 54–93). Hershey, PA: IGI Global. doi:10.4018/978-1-4666-4765-7.ch004

Zardari, M. A., & Jung, L. T. (2016). Classification of File Data Based on Confidentiality in Cloud Computing using K-NN Classifier. *International Journal of Business Analytics, 3*(2), 61–78. doi:10.4018/IJBAN.2016040104

Zhang, C., Simon, J. C., & Lee, E. (2016). An Empirical Investigation of Decision Making in IT-Related Dilemmas: Impact of Positive and Negative Consequence Information. *Journal of Organizational and End User Computing, 28*(4), 73–90. doi:10.4018/JOEUC.2016100105

Zou, J., Wang, Y., & Orgun, M. A. (2015). Modeling Accountable Cloud Services Based on Dynamic Logic for Accountability. *International Journal of Web Services Research, 12*(3), 48–77. doi:10.4018/IJWSR.2015070103

# About the Authors

**Dmitry Korzun** received his B.Sc. (1997) and M.Sc (1999) degrees in Applied Mathematics and Computer Science from the Petrozavodsk State University (PetrSU, Russia). He received a Ph.D. degree in Physics and Mathematics from the St.-Petersburg State University (Russia) in 2002. He is an Associate Professor at Department of Computer Science of PetrSU (since 2003 and ongoing). He was Visiting Research Scientist at the Helsinki Institute for Information Technology HIIT, Aalto University, Finland (2005-2014). In 2014-2016 he performed the duties of Vice-dean for Research at Faculty of Mathematics and Information Technology of PetrSU. Since 2014 he has acted as Leading Research Scientist at PetrSU, originating research and development activity within fundamental and applied research projects on emerging topics in ubiquitous computing, smart spaces, and Internet technology. Dmitry Korzun serves on technical program committees and editorial boards of a number of international conferences and journals. His research interests include modeling and evaluation of distributed systems, mathematical modeling and concept engineering of cyber-physical systems, ubiquitous computing and smart spaces, Internet of Things and its applications, software engineering and programming methods, algorithm design and complexity, linear Diophantine analysis and its applications, theory of formal languages and parsing. His educational activity started in 1997 at the Faculty of Mathematics of PetrSU (now Institute of Mathematics and Information Technology). Since that time he has taught more than 20 study courses on hot topics in Computer Science, Applied Mathematics, Information and Communication Technology, and Software Engineering. He is an author and co-author of more than 150 research and educational publications.

**Alexey Kashevnik** received his B.Sc. (2003) and M.Sc (2005) degrees in automated systems for information processing and management from the Peter the Great St.Petersburg Polytechnic University, Russia. He received a

Ph.D. degree in system analysis, information processing and management from the St.Petersburg Institute for Informatics and Automation of the Russian Academy of Sciences (SPIIRAS, Russia) in 2008. He is Senior Research Scientist at Laboratory of computer aided integrated systems of SPIIRAS (since 2008 and ongoing). He is Associate Professor at information technologies and management department of ITMO University, Russia. He was Associate Professor in Petrozavodsk State University (PetrSU, Russia) in 2015-2016. Alexey Kashevnik serves on technical program committees and editorial boards of a number of international conferences and journals. His research interests include smart spaces, Internet of Things and its applications, robotics, knowledge management, context management, profiling, clod systems, competence management, and advanced driver assistance systems. His research activity started in 2003 at the SPIIRAS. Since that time he is an author and co-author of more than 150 research and educational publications.

**Sergey Balandin** received M.Sc. degrees in Computer Science from Saint Petersburg Electrotechnical University "LETI" (Russia) and in Telecommunications from Lappeenranta University of Technology (Finland). His Ph.D. in Telecommunications and Control Theory was awarded in 2003by PhD school of Nokia Research Center and Saint Petersburg Electrotechnical University "LETI". He also received M.Sc. in Business Administration (MBA) from Haaga-Helia University of Applied Sciences (2012). From 1999 till 2011 Sergey worked in Nokia Research Center. His last position was Principal Scientist of Ubiquities Architectures team, Nokia's Academy cooperation manager for Russia and CIS and acting Technical Director of Nokia Siemens Networks in Russia. For three years he was Nokia representative in MIPI standardization Alliance, UniPro working group. Sergey Balandin is a serial entrepreneur in the innovative information technology sector. He is Adjunct Professor at the Department of Communications Engineering of Tampere University of Technology. He holds a number of positions of trust including General Chair position of Open Innovations Association FRUCT. He is IARIA Fellow (since 2011). Sergey Balandin is Editor-in-Chief of International Journal of Embedded and Real-Time Communication Systems (IJERTCS). Sergey holds position of invited Professor of ITMO University. He is an official expert of Skolkovo Foundation and EURIPIDES[2] program (ID 112). Sergey Balandin is an author of 29 patents and over 100 papers. He edited several proceedings and books published by LNCS, IEEE, and IGI. His research interests include Smart Spaces, Internet of Things, Embedded Networks and Smart Systems, and design of digital services.

# Index

Stay Current on the Latest Emerging Research Developments

# Become an IGI Global Reviewer for Authored Book Projects

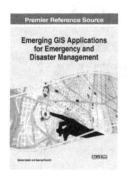

Premier Reference Source

Emerging GIS Applications for Emergency and Disaster Management

Premier Reference Source

Managerial Strategies and Green Solutions for Project Sustainability

Premier Reference Source

Comparative Approaches to Using R and Python for Statistical Data Analysis

Premier Reference Source

Solutions for High-Touch Communications in a High-Tech World

## The overall success of an authored book project is dependent on quality and timely reviews.

In this competitive age of scholarly publishing, constructive and timely feedback significantly decreases the turnaround time of manuscripts from submission to acceptance, allowing the publication and discovery of progressive research at a much more expeditious rate. Several IGI Global authored book projects are currently seeking highly qualified experts in the field to fill vacancies on their respective editorial review boards:

## Applications may be sent to:
### development@igi-global.com

Applicants must have a doctorate (or an equivalent degree) as well as publishing and reviewing experience. Reviewers are asked to write reviews in a timely, collegial, and constructive manner. All reviewers will begin their role on an ad-hoc basis for a period of one year, and upon successful completion of this term can be considered for full editorial review board status, with the potential for a subsequent promotion to Associate Editor.

If you have a colleague that may be interested in this opportunity, we encourage you to share this information with them.

Printed in the United States
By Bookmasters